PEOPLE YOU SHOULD KNOW

TOP 101 PHILOSOPHERS

Edited by Jeanne Nagle

Britannica
— Educational Publishing —

IN ASSOCIATION WITH

ROSEN
EDUCATIONAL SERVICES

Published in 2014 by Britannica Educational Publishing (a trademark of Encyclopædia Britannica, Inc.) in association with The Rosen Publishing Group, Inc.
29 East 21st Street, New York, NY 10010

Distributed exclusively by Rosen Publishing.
To see additional Britannica Educational Publishing titles, go to rosenpublishing.com

First Edition

Britannica Educational Publishing
J.E. Luebering: Director, Core Reference Group
Anthony L. Green: Editor, Compton's by Britannica

Rosen Publishing
Hope Lourie Killcoyne: Executive Editor
Jeanne Nagle: Editor
Nelson Sá: Art Director
Brian Garvey: Designer, cover design
Cindy Reiman: Photography Manager
Karen Huang: Photo Researcher

Library of Congress Cataloging-in-Publication Data

Top 101 philosophers / [editor] Jeanne Nagle. — First edition.
     pages cm — (People you should know)
Includes bibliographical references and index.
ISBN 978-1-62275-132-7 (library binding)
1. Philosophers—Biography—Juvenile literature. I. Nagle, Jeanne. II. Title: Top one hundred and one philosophers.
B104.T67 2014
109.2—dc23
[B]

                                                            2013033327

Manufactured in the United States of America

On the cover: Pictured are (top, left to right) Plato *Nick Paviakis/Shutterstock.com*; Simone de Beauvoir *Hulton Archive/Getty Images*; Aristotle *Panos Karas/Shutterstock.com*; Noam Chomsky *fotostory/Shutterstock.com*; (bottom, left to right) Jean-Paul Sartre *Keystone-France/ Gamma/Keystone/Getty Images*; Fredreich Nietzsche *Nicku/Shutterstock.com*; Bertrand Russell *Keystone-France/Gamma/Keystone/Getty Images*; and Confucius *Philip Lange/Shutterstock. com*.

Cover and interior pages (top) © iStockphoto.com/René Mansi

CONTENTS

8

24

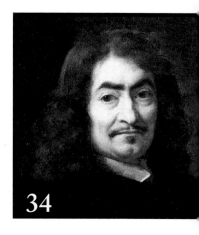

34

50

73

85

INTRODUCTION

Theories of existence, knowledge, and ethics have been advanced and argued since the time of the ancient Greeks. In the pages of this book, readers will discover more about the ideas that shaped the history of philosophy by examining the lives of the men—and women—who gave birth to those ideas.

Some of the earliest philosophers attributed human existence to the natural elements: earth, air, fire, and water. The Greek philosopher Heracleitus thought it was fire that was the essential material uniting all things, while Democritus found the basis of life in an element of a different kind—the atom. (He had unknowingly discovered the foundation of modern physics). Other philosophers have claimed that the basis of all things is not elements, but mathematics. Pythagoras surmised that numbers gave an underlying harmony and order to everything in existence.

When it comes to answering the question of existence, philosophy and religion have often overlapped, using philosophy to either prove or disprove the existence of a supreme being. St. Augustine claimed that it is only through the contemplation of, and connection with, God that humans can find real happiness. To the contrary, Danish philosopher and theologian Søren Kierkegaard essentially called faith irrational and said people should take personal responsibility for their own destinies rather than simply follow the flock.

The more philosophers pondered, the more they realized how little they actually understood. This led to questioning the very origins of knowledge. Socrates was a firm believer that people didn't know as much as they claimed they did. Using what is known as the Socratic method, he asked his students questions such as "What is knowledge?" or "What is virtue?" Then he would poke holes in their responses until they questioned their own understanding of the topic.

How we obtain knowledge also has been the subject of some debate among philosophers. While Plato believed that people are born with some knowledge of an ideal reality (and it is the philosophers' job to show them how to live in accordance with that reality), John Locke felt that babies are merely blank slates waiting to be filled with the knowledge gained from experience and observation. Francis Bacon agreed with the importance of observation. In fact, he suggested that every philosopher who had come before him had been wrong by focusing on words rather than on experimentation. Bacon's empirical approach to knowledge formed the foundation of the modern scientific method.

Philosophical investigation also tackles the question of ethics, or put simply, deciding what is right and what is wrong. The Scottish philosopher David Hume said that good and evil are derived from pleasure or pain. German Philosopher Friedrich Nietzsche thought that people should throw out the ideas of good and evil as mere conventions and instead create their own individual value systems. Some philosophers, among them a member of the French Enlightenment named Jean-Jacques Rousseau, felt that human nature is inherently good, but people become corrupted when they stifle their natural desires to fit within the confines of society's rules and order, ultimately leading to bad behavior.

These and the other great thinkers whose lives and beliefs are detailed in these pages have helped give shape and depth to human existence. And yet philosophy is a constantly evolving science. Just as some questions are addressed, new questions emerge. Expect the list of influential philosophers to grow over the years as people continue to probe and wonder about the great mysteries of the universe and human existence.

PETER ABELARD

(b. 1079 –d. 1142)

Peter Abelard was born in 1079, in Le Pallet, near Nantes, Brittany (now in France). He was a French theologian and philosopher best known for his solution of the problem of universals and for his original use of dialectics. He is also known for his poetry and for his celebrated love affair with a pupil named Heloise.

The outline of Abelard's career is well known, largely because he described so much of it in his famous *Historia calamitatum* ("History of My Troubles"). He was born the son of a knight in Brittany south of the Loire River. He sacrificed his inheritance and the prospect of a military career in order to study philosophy, particularly logic, in France. He provoked bitter quarrels with two of his masters, Roscelin of Compiègne and Guillaume de Champeaux, who represented opposite poles of philosophy in regard to the question of the existence of universals.

In 1113 or 1114 he went north to Laon to study theology under Anselm of Laon, the leading biblical scholar of the day, but soon returned to Paris. There he taught openly but was also given as a private pupil the young Heloise, niece of one of the clergy of the cathedral of Paris, Canon Fulbert. Abelard and Heloise fell in love and had a son whom they called Astrolabe. They then married secretly. Abelard suffered castration at Fulbert's instigation. In shame he embraced the monastic life at the royal abbey of Saint-Denis near Paris and made the unwilling Heloise become a nun at Argenteuil.

At Saint-Denis Abelard extended his reading in theology and tirelessly criticized the way of life followed by his fellow monks. His reading of the Bible and of the Fathers of the Church led him to make a collection of quotations that seemed to represent inconsistencies in the teachings of the Christian church. He arranged his findings in a compilation entitled *Sic et non* ("Yes and No") He also wrote the first version of his book called *Theologia*, which was formally condemned as heretical and burned by a council held at Soissons in 1121.

1

Portrait of Peter Abelard, taken from an illustrated book on the lives of famous Frenchmen by Edouard Mennechet. Leemage/Universal Images Group/ Getty Images

When he returned to Saint-Denis he applied his dialectical methods to the subject of the abbey's patron saint; he argued that St. Denis of Paris, the martyred apostle of Gaul, was not identical with Denis of Athens (also known as Dionysius the Areopagite), the convert of St. Paul. The monastic community of Saint-Denis regarded this criticism of their traditional claims as derogatory to the kingdom; and, in order to avoid being brought for trial before the king of France, Abelard fled from the abbey and sought asylum in the territory of Count Theobald of Champagne. There he sought the solitude of a hermit's life but was pursued by students who pressed him to resume his teaching in philosophy. His combination of the teaching of secular arts with his profession as a monk was heavily criticized by other men of religion, and Abelard contemplated flight outside Christendom altogether. In 1125, however, he accepted election as abbot of the remote Breton monastery of Saint-Gildas-de-Rhuys. There, too, his relations with the community deteriorated, and, after attempts had been made upon his life, he returned to France.

Heloise had meanwhile become the head of a new foundation of nuns called the Paraclete. Abelard became the abbot of the new community. He provided it with a rule and with a justification of the nun's way of life and in this he emphasized the virtue of literary study. He

2

also provided books of hymns he had composed, and in the early 1130s he and Heloise composed a collection of their own love letters and religious correspondence.

Around the year 1135 Abelard went to the Mont-Sainte-Geneviève outside Paris to teach, and he wrote in a blaze of energy and of celebrity. He produced further drafts of his *Theologia*. He also wrote a book called *Ethica* or *Scito te ipsum* ("Know Thyself"), a short masterpiece in which he analyzed the notion of sin and reached the drastic conclusion that human actions do not make a man better or worse in the sight of God. Abelard also wrote *Dialogus inter philosophum, Judaeum et Christianum* ("Dialogue Between a Philosopher, a Jew, and a Christian") and a commentary on St. Paul's letter to the Romans, *the Expositio in Epistolam ad Romanos*, in which he outlined an explanation of the purpose of Christ's life, which was to inspire men to love him by example alone.

Within Paris the influential abbey of Saint-Victor was studiously critical of his doctrines, while elsewhere William of Saint-Thierry, a former admirer of Abelard, recruited the support of Bernard of Clairvaux, perhaps the most influential figure in Western Christendom at that time. At a council held at Sens in 1140, Abelard underwent a resounding condemnation, which was soon confirmed by Pope Innocent II. He withdrew to the great monastery of Cluny in Burgundy. There, under the skillful mediation of the abbot, Peter the Venerable, he made peace with Bernard of Clairvaux and retired from teaching. Now both sick and old, he lived the life of a Cluniac monk. After his death, his body was first sent to the Paraclete where it now lies alongside that of Heloise in the cemetery of Père-Lachaise in Paris. Abelard died on April 21, 1142, at the Priory of Saint-Marcel, near Chalon-sur-Saône, Burgundy.

THEODOR ADORNO

(b. 1903–d. 1969)

Theodor Adorno was born Sep. 11, 1903, in Frankfurt, Ger. One of the most famous members of the Frankfurt School, Adorno deeply influenced postwar philosophy and the formation of critical theory. Besides his contribution to philosophy, Adorno also wrote books and treatises on aesthetics, musicology, and sociology.

Adorno studied philosophy at the Johann Wolfgang Goethe University and in 1924, received a degree in philosophy. Adorno then moved to the University of Frankfurt to teach philosophy. With Hitler's rise to power and his increased persecution of Jews, Adorno had no choice but to immigrate to England from his beloved Germany. Adorno taught at the University of Oxford for about three years and then moved to Princeton University in the United States in 1938. Adorno later went to the University of California, Berkeley, where he would spend the next seven years.

In 1949, Adorno and his colleague at the Frankfurt School, Max Horkheimer, returned to Frankfurt. They revived the Frankfurt School, and rebuilt the Institute for Social Research together at the University of Frankfurt. The Institute became a focal point in the western world for studies and research in socialism. However, Adorno deviated from his traditional Marxist viewpoint when he argued after his return to Frankfurt that besides the effect of economics, social and cultural variables also come into play in the mechanics of oppression.

One of Adorno's most significant books was the *Dialectic of Enlightenment*, coauthored with his friend and kindred spirit, Max Horkheimer. The book explores the human tendency to self-destruct and the rise and causes of Fascism, as well as the death of freedom. Adorno argued that the answer lay in aesthetics and not in rationalization. The chapter "The Culture Industry," in *Dialectic of Enlightenment* became notorious for its proposition that popular culture was in effect mass production of what Adorno and Horkheimer termed as "cultural goods."

Adorno died on Aug. 6, 1969, in Visp, Swit. His other seminal work, *The Aesthetic Theory,* was published a few months after Adorno passed away. In this book, Adorno described the cohabiting of art and philosophy, and his view on what the "character of art" could be. Adorno also wrote *Philosophie der neuen Musik* (1949; *Philosophy of Modern Music*), *The Authoritarian Personality* (1950, in collaboration) and *Negative Dialektik* (1966; *Negative Dialectics*).

SAINT ANSELM OF CANTERBURY

(b. 1033?–d. 1109)

St. Anselm was born at Aosta, Italy, in about 1033. In the late Middle Ages the attempt to use philosophy to explain Christian faith was called scholasticism. The founder of scholasticism was St. Anselm, a philosopher, theologian, monk, and archbishop.

In his youth he resisted family pressure to enter politics and obtained a classical education instead. In 1057 he entered the Benedictine monastery at Bec, in northwestern France. In 1078 he became the abbot there. As Anselm's abilities and great learning became known, Bec became one of the leading schools of philosophy and theology.

While on inspection tours of monasteries in England, Anselm had been befriended by King William I. In 1093 William I's son and successor, William II Rufus, appointed Anselm archbishop of Canterbury. His term of office was an unhappy one, for he immediately became involved in one of the major conflicts of the time—the investiture controversy: at issue was whether a king had the right to invest a bishop with the symbols of his office. On this issue Anselm resisted both William II and his successor, Henry I. The matter was finally resolved in Anselm's favor by the Westminster Agreement of 1107. He lived only two more years, dying on April 21, 1109.

Anselm is remembered principally as one of the great theologians in the history of the Roman Catholic Church. His main works—the *Monologium* (*Monologue*), the *Proslogium* (*Addition*), and the *Cur Deus Homo?* (*Why Did God Become Man?*)—were outstanding attempts to use reason to explain belief. He was canonized as a saint in 1163 and declared a doctor of the Church in 1720.

HANNAH ARENDT

(b. 1906–d. 1975)

Hannah Arendt was born on Oct. 14, 1906, in Hannover, Ger. She was a German-born American political scientist and philosopher

5

known for her critical writing on Jewish affairs and her study of totalitarianism.

Arendt grew up in Hannover, Ger., and in Königsberg, Prussia (now Kaliningrad, Russia). Beginning in 1924 she studied philosophy at the Universities of Marburg, Freiburg, and Heidelberg where she received a doctoral degree in philosophy in 1928. At Marburg she began a romantic relationship with her teacher, Martin Heidegger, which lasted until 1928. In 1933, when Heidegger joined the Nazi Party and began implementing Nazi educational policies as rector of Freiburg, Arendt, who was Jewish, was forced to flee to Paris. She married Heinrich Blücher, a philosophy professor, in 1940. She again became a fugitive from the Nazis in 1941, when she and her husband immigrated to the United States.

Settling in New York City, she became research director of the Conference on Jewish Relations (1944–46), chief editor of Schocken Books (1946–48), and executive director (1949–52) of Jewish Cultural Reconstruction, Inc., which sought to salvage Jewish writings dispersed by the Nazis. She was naturalized as an American citizen in 1951. She taught at the University of Chicago from 1963 to 1967 and thereafter at the New School for Social Research in New York City.

Arendt's reputation as a major political thinker was established by her *Origins of Totalitarianism* (1951). *The Human Condition*, published in 1958, was a wide-ranging and systematic treatment of what Arendt called the vita activa (Latin: "active life"). Like most of her work, it owed a great deal to the philosophical style of Heidegger.

In a highly controversial work, *Eichmann in Jerusalem* (1963), based on her reportage of the trial of the Nazi war criminal Adolf Eichmann in 1961, Arendt argued that Eichmann's crimes resulted not from a wicked character but from sheer "thoughtlessness." Arendt's refusal to recognize Eichmann as "inwardly" evil sparked off furious criticism from both Jewish and non-Jewish intellectuals.

Arendt resumed contact with Heidegger in 1950, and in subsequent essays and lectures she defended him by claiming that his Nazi involvement had been the "mistake" of a great philosopher. In the late 20th century, following the publication of a volume of letters between Arendt and Heidegger written between 1925 and 1975, some scholars suggested that Arendt's personal and intellectual attachment to her former teacher had led her to be lenient in her assessment of him.

Arendt's other works include *Between Past and Future* (1961), *On Revolution* (1963), *Men in Dark Times* (1968), *On Violence* (1970), and *Crises of the Republic* (1972). Her unfinished manuscript *The Life of the Mind* was edited by her friend and correspondent Mary McCarthy and published in 1978. *Responsibility and Judgment*, published in 2003, collects essays and lectures on moral topics from the years following publication of *Eichmann in Jerusalem*. Arendt died on Dec. 4, 1975, in New York City.

ARISTOTLE
(b. 384 BCE–d. 322 BCE)

One of the greatest thinkers of all time was Aristotle, an ancient Greek philosopher. His work in the natural and social sciences greatly influenced almost every area of modern thinking.

Aristotle was born in 384 BCE in Stagira, on the northwest coast of the Aegean Sea. His father was a friend and the physician of the king of Macedonia, and he spent most of his boyhood at the court. At 17, Aristotle went to Athens to study. He enrolled at the famous Academy directed by the philosopher Plato.

Aristotle threw himself wholeheartedly into Plato's pursuit of truth and goodness. Plato was soon calling him the "mind of the school." Aristotle stayed at the Academy for 20 years, leaving only when his beloved master died in 347 BCE. In later years he renounced some of Plato's theories and went far beyond him in breadth of knowledge.

Aristotle became a teacher in a school on the coast of Asia Minor. He spent two years studying marine biology on Lesbos. In 342 BCE, Philip II invited Aristotle to return to the Macedonian court and teach his 13-year-old son Alexander. This was the boy who was to become conqueror of the world. No one knows how much influence the philosopher had on the headstrong youth. After Alexander became king, at 20, he gave his teacher a large sum of money to set up a school in Athens.

Bust of the ancient Greek philosopher Aristotle. Photos.com

In Athens, Aristotle taught brilliantly at his school in the Lyceum. He collected the first great library and established a museum. In the mornings he strolled in the Lyceum gardens, discussing problems with his advanced students.

Aristotle walked about while teaching and for this reason Athenians called his school the Peripatetic (which means "to walk about") school. He led his pupils in research in every existing field of knowledge.

One of Aristotle's most important contributions was defining and classifying the various branches of knowledge. He sorted them into physics, metaphysics, psychology, rhetoric, poetics, and logic, and thus laid the foundation of most of the sciences of today.

Anti-Macedonian feeling broke out in Athens in 323 BCE. The Athenians accused Aristotle of being immoral. He chose to flee, so that the Athenians might not "twice sin against philosophy" (by killing him as they had Socrates). He fled to Chalcis on the island of Euboea. There he died the next year.

After his death, Aristotle's writings were scattered or lost. In the early Middle Ages the only works of his known in Western Europe were parts of his writings on logic. They became the basis of one of the three subjects of the medieval trio—logic, grammar, and rhetoric. Early in the 13th century other books reached the West. Some came from Constantinople; others were brought by the Arabs to Spain. Medieval scholars translated them into Latin.

The best known of Aristotle's writings that have been preserved are *Organon* (treatises on logic), *Rhetoric, Poetics, History of Animals,*

8

Metaphysics, *De Anima* (on psychology), *Nicomachean Ethics*, *Politics*, and *Constitution of Athens*.

SAINT AUGUSTINE OF HIPPO

(b. 354– d. 430)

The bishop of Hippo in Roman Africa for 35 years, St. Augustine lived during the decline of Roman civilization on that continent. Considered the greatest of the Fathers of the Church in the West, he helped form Christian theology.

Augustine was born Aurelius Augustinus on Nov. 13, 354, at Tagaste in the Roman province of Numidia (now Souk-Ahras in Algeria). Although his mother, St. Monica, was a devout Christian, he was not baptized in infancy. His father, Patricius, a wealthy landowner, was a pagan.

In his *Confessions* Augustine wrote seven chapters about an incident in his early life—stealing pears from a neighbor's tree. This sin troubled him for the rest of his life. He also confessed to immoral behavior at the University of Carthage, where he was sent at the age of 16.

Augustine remained in Carthage, teaching rhetoric, until he was 29. Then he went to Rome, taking with him his mistress and his son, Adeodatus. His religion at this time was Manichaeism, which combined Christianity with Zoroastrian elements.

By 386 Augustine was teaching in Milan, where his mother joined him. He came under the influence of the city's great bishop, St. Ambrose, who baptized Augustine and Adeodatus on the following Easter.

From this time Augustine lived as an ascetic. He returned to Africa and spent three years with friends on his family's estate. He was ordained a priest and five years later, in 396, was consecrated a bishop.

Augustine's most widely read book is *Confessions*, a vivid account of his early life and religious development. *The City of God* was written after 410, when Rome fell to the barbarians. The aim of this book was to restore confidence in the Christian Church, which Augustine said would take the place of the earthly city of Rome. During the Middle Ages the book gave strong support to the theory that the Church was above the state. Augustine's writings on communal life form the Rule of St. Augustine, the basis of many religious orders.

He spent the remainder of his life in Hippo (now Annaba, Alg.) with his clergy, encouraging the formation of religious communities. Augustine, who was ill when the Vandals besieged Hippo, died on Aug. 28, 430, before the town was taken.

AVERROES

(b. 1126–d. 1198)

One of the major Islamic scholars of the Middle Ages, Averroes wrote observations on the Greek philosophers Plato and Aristotle. These works contributed significantly to the development of both Jewish and Christian thought in subsequent centuries.

Averroes was born in Córdoba, Spain, in 1126. He was very well educated in Muslim science, medicine, philosophy, and law. He became chief judge at Córdoba and personal physician to the city rulers.

Between 1169 and 1195 Averroes wrote a series of commentaries on most of Aristotle's works and on Plato's *Republic*. His penetrating mind enabled him to present the thought of these philosophers efficiently and to add considerably to its understanding.

Averroes wrote several original works. His first book, *General Medicine*, was written from 1162 to 1169. Three religious-philosophical treatises written in 1179 to 1180 have survived, but most of his legal works and all his theological books have been lost. He died at Marrakesh in North Africa in 1198.

AVICENNA

(b. 980–d. 1037)

During the Middle Ages, few scholars contributed more to science and philosophy than the Muslim scholar Avicenna. By his writings he helped convey the thoughts of the Greek philosopher Aristotle to the thinkers of Western Europe, and his *Canon of Medicine* became the definitive work in its field for centuries.

Born in Bukhara, Persia (now in Iran), in 980, he spent his childhood and youth studying Islamic law, literature, and medicine. By age 21 he was considered a great scholar and an outstanding physician.

After his father's death, Avicenna left Bukhara and for about twenty years lived in different Persian cities, working as a physician and completing two of his major works. *The Book of Healing* was a large encyclopedia covering the natural sciences, logic, mathematics, psychology, astronomy, music, and philosophy. It is probably the largest work of its kind ever written by one man. The *Canon of Medicine* was a systematic exposition of the achievements of Greek and Roman physicians.

Portrait of Avicenna, a philosopher and physician who flourished in the Middle Ages. Image from the History of Medicine, National Library of Medicine

For the last 14 years of his life, Avicenna lived in the city of Isfahan and continued his prodigious writing career. He died in 1037.

In the next century much of Avicenna's work was translated into Latin and thereby became available to the philosophers and theologians of Europe. In Islam his contributions to medicine, theology, and philosophy are still recognized as valuable.

A.J. AYER

(b. 1910–d. 1989)

Sir Alfred Jules Ayer was born in London in 1910. He was a British philosopher and specialized in linguistic analysis. Ayer attended Eton College and Oxford and spent most of his teaching career at Oxford.

Ayer was a proponent of logical positivism and a member of the British intelligence corps during World War II. His best-known book is *Language, Truth, and Logic* (1936) and his other works include *Foundations of Empirical Knowledge* (1940), *The Problem of Knowledge* (1956), and *The Central Questions of Philosophy* (1973). Ayer was knighted in 1970.

FRANCIS BACON

(b. 1561–d. 1626)

Historians have found Francis Bacon a fascinating subject. He gained fame as a speaker in Parliament and as a lawyer in some famous trials. He also served as Lord Chancellor of England under King James I. As a philosopher and writer, Bacon attempted to explain the principles of acquiring knowledge. Because he tried to write while holding public office that demanded much time and attention, many of his works remained fragments. The writings that have been preserved have marked him as an innovative thinker.

In all, Bacon wrote more than 30 philosophical works and many legal, popular, scientific, historical, and other books and essays. His popular literature is noted most for the worldly wisdom of a few dozen essays. He laid out a plan for the reorganization of knowledge into categories in his *Novum Organum* (1620), the second volume of an ambitious six-part series. But he never finished the *Novum Organum* or his larger project, though parts of four of the other books have survived. Among the latter is *The Advancement of Learning* (1605), considered with *Novum Organum* as Bacon's main philosophical work.

Francis Bacon was born on Jan. 22, 1561, in London. The second son of Sir Nicholas Bacon, keeper of the royal seal, Bacon grew up familiar with the royal court. His mother, Ann Cooke, was famous for her learning. Bacon went to study at Trinity College, Cambridge, at the age of 12. He lived in Paris, France, from 1576 until his father's death in 1579.

Bacon began a legal education on his return to London in 1579. He was admitted to the bar as a barrister in 1582 and later became a reader or lecturer at Gray's Inn, a London institution for legal education. But the law failed to satisfy his desire to follow a political and intellectual career.

His skill as a public speaker served Bacon well when he took a seat in the House of Commons in 1584. He found it difficult to gain political influence even though his uncle was Lord Burghley, first minister to Queen Elizabeth I. He wrote a *Letter of Advice to Queen Elizabeth* in 1584 or 1585, recommending ways to deal with Roman Catholic subjects, and *An Advertisement Touching the Controversies of the Church of England* (1589) in which he attacked what he saw as religious abuses.

Bacon was becoming famous but still wanted higher offices. With the accession of James I to the English throne in 1603, Bacon's fortunes improved. He held a succession of posts, including those of Solicitor General and Attorney General. In the growing controversies between James and Parliament, Bacon defended the rights of the monarchy. He was knighted in 1603 and became Lord Chancellor and Baron Verulam in 1618 and Viscount St. Albans in 1621.

His political enemies brought about his downfall, charging him with bribery and other offenses. He was fined and imprisoned briefly in the Tower of London. Barred from public office, he retired to his estate at Gorhambury.

A fine writer, Bacon contributed to the scientific revolution of the 17th century. He neglected the role of mathematics in science, but advised students of nature to follow the rule that "whatever the mind seizes and dwells upon with particular satisfaction is to be held in suspicion." He felt deeply that science held the key to technological progress.

Bacon holds a prominent place in literature and philosophy. But the fragmentary nature of his writings makes it difficult to assess his stature. He often attempted more than he could finish. In addition to his incomplete *Novum Organum*, he planned six volumes of natural history, but completed only two. In 1610 he published *The New Atlantis*, a fiction work on the ideal state. But his great effort, the plan for the renewal of knowledge that was entitled *Instauratio Magna* (*Great Renewal*), was also left incomplete. Bacon died at Highgate on April 9, 1626.

SIMONE DE BEAUVOIR

(b. 1908– d. 1986)

Philosopher and writer Simone de Beavoir, whose work was a precursor to modern feminist theory. Hulton Archive/Getty Images

Simone de Beavior was born in Paris on Jan. 9, 1908. An exponent of existentialism, Simone de Beauvoir became an internationally respected philosopher and writer, through her novels, essays, and memoirs. Her 1949 landmark study *Le Deuxième sexe* (in English, *The Second Sex*, 1953), translated and read around the world, became one of the principal engines of the modern women's movement everywhere.

Simone Lucie Ernestine Marie Bertrand de Beauvoir had a conventional middle class upbringing against which she rebelled while

14

studying at the École Normale Supérieure to become a teacher. It was there that she met the philosopher Jean-Paul Sartre, and she ranked second behind him in their graduating class. Attracted to Sartre's intellectual brilliance and non-conformism, they formed a relationship that endured until Sartre's death. After graduating, de Beauvoir became a teacher in Marseille, Rouen, and Paris before publishing her first novel, *L'Invitée* (published in English as *She Came to Stay*), in 1943. Through Sartre, she was introduced to the intellectual circles she depicted in *The Mandarins*, the novel that won the 1954 Prix Goncourt. Meanwhile, her essays had established her as a leading figure in French intellectual life. "You are not born a woman, you become one," Simone de Beauvoir wrote in *The Second Sex*, a work that set the agenda for the women's liberation movement and that, with its emphasis on the individual in relation to the other, gave a new and highly productive direction to the existentialist philosophy of Sartre.

Increasingly, de Beauvoir's search for the root of women's alienation in a male-dominated society took her back to her own experience, and her account of this in her memoirs, starting with *Mémoires d'une jeune fille rangée* (*Memoirs of a Dutiful Daughter*) in 1958, is highly personal and thoughtful analysis of French society. *Une Mort très douce* (*A Very Easy Death*; 1964), the devastating story of her mother's last illness and death, is a moving tribute from one woman to another, both from different generations.

It was perhaps inevitable that de Beauvoir's feminine awareness should make her ideas differ from Sartre's. Hailed as one of the country's greatest writers, she was not merely the companion of his intellectual adventure. The reminiscences she published after his death, starting in 1982 with *La Cérémonie des adieux* (*Adieux: A Farewell to Sartre*), shocked some of Sartre's admirers by their frank revelations of his final years. However, uncompromising honesty was the hallmark of her work, and there had never been any likelihood that she would retire into the role of the idolizing "widow" of the man who had been her closest personal and literary associate for more than 50 years. She died on April 14, 1986, in Paris.

JEREMY BENTHAM

(b. 1748–d. 1832)

Jeremy Bentham was born in London on Feb. 15, 1748. In explaining his ideas of the useful and the good, Bentham became the first utilitarian. His philosophy, called utilitarianism, holds that all human actions must be judged by their usefulness in promoting the greatest happiness for the greatest number of persons. Bentham also wrote on economics, politics, judicial and legislative institutions, and other subjects.

Bentham studied at Queen's College, Oxford, graduating at age 15. Beginning in 1763 he studied law in London, later joining the King's Bench division of the High Court. There he came under the influence of Lord William Mansfield, an important jurist. But Bentham soon lost interest in studying to practice law. Instead, he conducted chemical experiments and speculated on legal theory.

Bentham's first book, *A Fragment on Government* (1776), was a critical analysis of portions of Sir William Blackstone's *Commentaries on the Laws of England* (1765–69). Bentham wrote that Blackstone's chief error was his resistance to reform. Bentham next wrote *Théorie des peines et des recompenses* (1811), which appeared in English in two parts as *The Rationale of Reward* (1825) and *The Rationale of Punishment* (1830). An essay on economics, *Defence of Usury* (1787) was written after a visit to Russia. In the book, Bentham advocated free enterprise economics. In *An Introduction to the Principles of Morals and Legislation* (1789) he described his utilitarian theories and how they could be used to reform law codes.

Bentham defined utility as "that property in any object whereby it tends to produce pleasure, good, or happiness, or to prevent the happening of mischief, pain, evil, or unhappiness to the party whose interest is considered. " He wrote that, since all punishment involves pain and is therefore evil, it ought to be used by the law only "so far as it promises to exclude some greater evil." Bentham's work inspired many law reforms, especially regarding prisons. He died on June 6, 1832, in London.

HENRI BERGSON

(b. 1859–d. 1941)

Henri-Louis Bergson was born on Oct. 18, 1859 in Paris. He was a French philosopher, the first to elaborate what came to be called "aprocess philosophy." He was also a master literary stylist, of both academic and popular appeal, and was awarded the Nobel Prize for Literature in 1927.

Bergson was descended from a rich Polish Jewish family and his upbringing, training, and interests were typically French. His professional career, as indeed all of his life, was spent in France, most of it in Paris.

Bergson received his early education at the Lycée Condorcet in Paris, where he showed equally great intelligence in the sciences and the humanities. From 1878 to 1881 he studied at the École Normale Supérieure in Paris. His teaching career began in various lycées outside of Paris, first at Angers (1881–83) and then for the next five years at Clermont-Ferrand. While at the latter place, he had the intuition that provided both the basis and inspiration for his first philosophical books.

Bergson first wrote *Essai sur les données immédiates de la conscience* (1889; *Time and Free Will: An Essay on the Immediate Data of Consciousness*), for which he received his doctorate the same year. This work was primarily an attempt to establish the notion of duration, or lived time, as opposed to what Bergson viewed as the spatialized conception of time measured by a clock that is used by science.

After the publication of the *Essai*, Bergson returned to Paris, teaching at the Lycée Henri IV. In 1891 he married Louise Neuburger, a cousin of the French novelist Marcel Proust. Meanwhile, he had undertaken the study of the relation between mind and body. Though he was convinced that he had successfully answered the argument for determinism,

17

his own work, in his doctoral dissertation, had not attempted to explain how mind and body are related. The findings of his research into this problem were published in 1896 under the title *Matière et mémoire: essai sur la relation du corps à l'esprit* (*Matter and Memory*).

This is the most difficult and perhaps also the most perfect of his books. The approach that he took in it is typical of his method of doing philosophy. For, *Matière et mémoire* he devoted five years to studying all of the literature available on memory and especially the psychological phenomenon of aphasia, or loss of the ability to use language. According to the theory of psychophysiological parallelism, a lesion in the brain should also affect the very basis of a psychological power. The occurrence of aphasia, Bergson argued, showed that this is not the case. The person so affected understands what others have to say, knows what he himself wants to say, suffers no paralysis of the speech organs, and yet is unable to speak. This fact shows, he argued, that it is not memory that is lost but, rather, the bodily mechanism that is needed to express it. From this observation Bergson concluded that memory, and so mind, or soul, is independent of body and makes use of it to carry out its own purposes.

The *Essai* had been widely reviewed in the professional journals, but *Matière et mémoire* attracted the attention of a wider audience and marked the first step along the way that led to Bergson's becoming one of the most popular and influential lecturers and writers of the day. In 1897 he returned as professor of philosophy to the École Normale Supérieure, which he had first entered as a student at the age of 19. Then, in 1900, he was called to the Collège de France, the academic institution of highest prestige in all of France, where he enjoyed immense success as a lecturer.

L'Évolution créatrice (1907; *Creative Evolution*), the greatest work of these years and Bergson's most famous book, reveals him most clearly as a philosopher of process at the same time that it shows the influence of biology upon his thought. He proposed that the whole evolutionary process should be seen as the endurance of an *élan vital* ("vital impulse") that is continually developing and generating new forms. Evolution, in short, is creative, not mechanical.

Among Bergson's minor works are *Le Rire: essai sur la significance du comique* (1900; *Laughter: An Essay on the Meaning of the Comic*) and, *Introduction à la metaphysique* (1903; *An Introduction to Metaphysics*). Bergson died on Jan. 4, 1941, in Paris.

GEORGE BERKELEY

(b. 1685–d. 1753)

George Berkeley was born in or near Kilkenny, Ire., on March 12, 1685. He was an Anglo-Irish bishop, philosopher, and scientist. George Berkeley felt that all matter, as humans know it, exists as a perception of mind. More broadly, he claimed everything except the spiritual exists only to the extent that it is viewed by humans. With this empiricist philosophy Berkeley challenged philosophers who said that matter is the only reality. His theory was misunderstood before the 20th century.

Berkeley attended Trinity College, Dublin. He earned a bachelor of arts degree in 1704. While awaiting a fellowship vacancy, he made a critical study of time, vision, and the hypothesis that there is no material substance. His first publication, *Arithmetica and Miscellanea Mathematica* (published together in 1707), was probably a fellowship thesis. Elected a fellow of Trinity College in 1707, Berkeley wrote his "Essay Towards a New Theory of Vision" (1709), stating that having ideas was simply the association of visual and other sensations. Berkeley spent about seven years in travels through France and Italy. He spent three years, 1729 to 1731, in America, encouraging higher education in the colonies. Returning to the British Isles, he became Bishop of Cloyne, in Ireland, and wrote on Irish social problems, philosophy, and scientific subjects.

Berkeley influenced later philosophers such as Immanuel Kant and Thomas Reid. Berkeley's development as a philosopher can be traced in his books. In Part I of his *Treatise Concerning the Principles of Human Knowledge* (1710), for example, he placed in the mind all objects perceived by any of the senses. His *Three Dialogues Between Hylas and Philonous*

(1713) extended the main arguments of his earlier book, *Principles*. *De Motu* (1721) attacked Sir Isaac Newton's theories of absolute space, time, and motion. *Alciphron or, the Minute Philosopher* (1732) was written during Berkeley's stay in America and it defended theism, the belief in God. Later works dealt with such diverse subjects as politics, economics, and science. Berkeley died in Oxford, Eng. on Jan. 14, 1753. In 1866 the city of Berkeley, Calif., was named after him.

BOETHIUS

(b. 470–475?–d. 524 CE?)

Boethius illustration from Andre Thevet's Vie Des Hommes Illustres, *published in 1584.* Hulton Archive /Getty Images

Anicius Manlius Severinus Boethius was born somewhere between 470–475 CE, probably in Rome. He was a Roman scholar, Christian philosopher, and statesman and author of the celebrated *De consolatione philosophiae (Consolation of Philosophy)*. This work was a largely Neo-platonic work in which the pursuit of wisdom and the love of God are described as the true sources of human happiness.

Boethius belonged to the ancient Roman family of the Anicii, which had been Christian for about a century and of which Emperor Olybrius had been a member. Boethius's father had been consul in 487 but died soon afterward, and Boethius was raised by Quintus Aurelius Memmius Symmachus, whose daughter Rusticiana he married. He became consul in 510 under the Ostrogothic king Theodoric. Although little of Boethius's education is known, he was evidently well trained in Greek. His early works on arithmetic and music still survive, both based on Greek handbooks by Nicomachus of Gerasa, a 1st-century-CE Palestinian mathematician. There is little that survives of Boethius's geometry, and there is nothing of his astronomy.

It was Boethius's scholarly aim to translate into Latin the complete works of Aristotle with commentary and all the works of Plato "perhaps with commentary," to be followed by a "restoration of their ideas into a single harmony." Boethius's dedicated Hellenism, modeled on Cicero's, supported his long labor of translating Aristotle's *Organon* (six treatises on logic) and the Greek glosses on the work.

Boethius had begun before 510 to translate Porphyry's *Eisagoge*, a 3rd-century Greek introduction to Aristotle's logic, and elaborated it in a double commentary. He then translated the *Katēgoriai*, wrote a commentary in 511 in the year of his consulship, and also translated and wrote two commentaries on the second of Aristotle's six treatises, the *Peri hermeneias* (*On Interpretation*). A brief ancient commentary on Aristotle's *Analytika Protera* (*Prior Analytics*) may be his too. He also wrote two short works on the syllogism.

About 520 Boethius put his close study of Aristotle to use in four short treatises in letter form on the ecclesiastical doctrines of the Trinity and the nature of Christ. Notwithstanding these works, doubt has at times been cast on Boethius's theological writings because in his logical works and in the later *Consolation* the Christian idiom is nowhere apparent. The 19th-century discovery of the biography written by Cassiodorus, however, confirmed Boethius as a Christian writer, even if his philosophic sources were non-Christian.

About 520 Boethius became *magister officiorum* (head of all the government and court services) under Theodoric. His two sons were consuls together in 522. Eventually Boethius fell out of favor with Theodoric. After the healing of a schism between Rome and the church of Constantinople in 520, Boethius and other senators were suspected of communicating with the Byzantine emperor Justin I. Sentence was passed and was ratified by the Senate, probably under duress. In prison, while he was awaiting execution, Boethius wrote his masterwork, *De consolatione philosophiae*.

When Cassiodorus founded a monastery at Vivarium, in Campania, he installed there his Roman library and included Boethius's works. Thus, some of the literary habits of the ancient aristocracy entered the monastic tradition. Boethian logic dominated the training of the medieval clergy and the work of the cloister and court schools. His translations and commentaries, particularly those of the *Katēgoriai* and *Peri hermeneias*, became basic texts in medieval Scholasticism. Translations of the *Consolation* appeared early in the great vernacular literatures, with King Alfred (9th century) and Chaucer (14th century) in English, Jean de Meun (a 13th-century poet) in French, and Notker Labeo (a monk of around the turn of the 11th century) in German. There was a Byzantine version in the 13th century by Planudes and a 16th-century English one by Elizabeth I.

After his detention, probably at Pavia, he was executed in 524. His remains were later placed in the church of San Pietro in Ciel d'Oro in Pavia, where, possibly through confusion with his namesake, St. Severinus of Noricum, they received the veneration due a martyr and a memorable salute from Dante.

MARTIN BUBER

(b. 1878–d. 1965)

B uber was born in Vienna, Austria, on Feb. 8, 1878, and was introduced early in life to Hasidism, the East European Jewish movement toward deeper piety. Raised in Russia by his grandfather, he studied philosophy and art at the universities of Vienna, Berlin, Leipzig, and Zurich. He founded the influential monthly *Der Jude* (*The Jew*) in 1916, remaining as editor until 1924. He became a Zionist, calling for a Jewish homeland.

A Jewish theologian, Biblical translator, and writer, Buber saw man as a being engaged continually in an encounter, or dialogue, with other beings. In this view the person has contacts with other people but has an ultimate relationship with God. The book *Ich und Du* (*I and Thou*), published in 1923, gave Buber's most detailed explanation of his beliefs. He held that God, the great Thou, makes possible the human I-Thou relationships between man and other beings. Man can have imperfect relationships with other beings—and sometimes, nearly perfect relationships, as in a deep friendship. But man commits the greatest evil of all when he refuses to move towards the I-Thou relationship with God. His views have influenced the work of several Protestant theologians.

Buber's philosophical writings hold that man and God have separate existences. In the continuing man-God encounter individuals face ethical problems daily: they must do the maximum of good and the minimum of evil if any is necessary. His independence of mind gave his Judaism a unique character. Combined with his belief in the need for a moderate policy toward the Arabs, his ideas set him apart from many of his own people. He discussed social problems in his book *Eclipse of God* (1952) and the evil of religious indifference in *Good and Evil* (1953). Because he opposed Nazi principles, the German government banned his public lectures in the 1930s. In 1938 he left Germany for Palestine. He died in Jerusalem in Israel on June 13, 1965.

RUDOLPH CARNAP

(b. 1891–d. 1970)

R udolph Carnap was a U.S. philosopher and a leading exponent of the school called Logical Positivism. Carnap was born in Ronsdorf, Ger. and he studied physics, mathematics, and philosophy at several German universities. He also taught at several universities, including Vienna, Prague, and Chicago.

Carnap was a founder of, *International Encyclopedia of Unified Science* and much of his study was devoted to logical analysis of language, logic, and probability. He published *Meaning and Necessity* in 1947 and *Logical Foundations of Probability* in 1950.

NOAM CHOMSKY

(b. 1928–d.)

Avram Noam Chomsky was born on Dec. 7, 1928, in Philadelphia. Chomsky once described his goal as a linguist as finding "the principles common to all languages that enable people to speak creatively and freely." He believed that children are born with an unconscious knowledge of the basic principles underlying all languages. Chomsky gave linguistics a new direction and strongly influenced the fields of philosophy and psychology. He was also influential as a leftist political activist.

Chomsky was introduced to linguistics by his father, a Hebrew scholar who worked with historical linguistics. Noam studied at the University of Pennsylvania, earning a bachelor's degree and then a master's. He followed it up with a junior fellowship at Harvard University in 1951–55. He received a doctorate in linguistics from the University of Pennsylvania in 1955 and then began teaching at the Massachusetts Institute of Technology.

Noam Chomsky, in his office at the Massachusetts Institute of Technology in the 1980s. Ulf Andersen/Hulton Archive/ Getty Images

At the time, the focus of linguistics in the United States was the study of speech sounds and how they are combined in various languages. Chomsky believed that it is less important to study the structures of different languages themselves than it is to study the mental structures common to speakers of all languages that allow them to learn the languages to which they are exposed as young children. He stressed that all children go through the same stages of language development regardless of the language they are learning. They also pick up the language spoken around them relatively quickly on their own, without much specific instruction. He thus believed that the proper focus of linguistics is to develop a theory of a universal grammar, an inborn faculty that allows young children to so easily acquire a rich knowledge of their language. Moreover, an understanding of this faculty can shed light on how the human brain is organized.

Chomsky also wrote and lectured widely on politics. A self-described libertarian socialist, he criticized what he considered to be the antidemocratic character of corporate power and its negative influence on U.S. foreign policy, domestic politics, and the mass media.

AUGUSTE COMTE

(b. 1798–d. 1857)

Auguste Comte was born in Montpellier, France, on Jan. 19, 1798. His father, Louis, was a tax official. Auguste studied at the École Polytechnique in Paris from 1814 to 1816. In 1818 he became secretary to the Comte de St-Simon, a pioneer socialist. Beginning in 1826, Comte delivered private lectures to some of the leading French scholars and scientists of his day. These lectures became the basis of his most famous work, the six-volume *Course of Positive Philosophy* which was published between 1830 and 1842. In 1827, two years after his marriage to Caroline Massin, Comte suffered a mental breakdown. After his recovery he was on the staff of the École Polytechnique from 1832 to 1842. In his four-volume *System of Positive Polity* published between 1851 and 1854 Comte formulated a concept called "religion of humanity."

Comte is best known for his "law of the three stages." According to this law, man's explanations of natural and social processes pass through three stages—the theological, the metaphysical, and the positive. In the first stage, man sees these processes as the work of supernatural powers. In the second, he explains them by means of such abstract ideas as "causes" and "forces."

In the third stage, he accumulates factual data and determines relationships among the observed facts. Comte believed that astronomy, physics, chemistry, and biology had evolved through these stages. He sought to organize sociology along "positive" lines. Comte died in Paris on Sept. 5, 1857.

MARQUIS DE CONDORCET

(b. 1743–d. 1794)

Marie-Jean-Antoine-Nicolas de Caritat, Marquis de Condorcet was born on Sept. 17, 1743, in Ribemont, France. He was a French philosopher of the Enlightenment and advocate of educational reform. He was one of the major Revolutionary formulators of the ideas of progress.

He was descended from the ancient family of Caritat, who took their title from Condorcet, a town in Dauphiné. He was educated at the Jesuit College in Reims and at the College of Navarre in Paris, where he showed his first promise as a mathematician. In 1769 he became a member of the Academy of Sciences, to which he contributed papers on mathematical and other subjects.

Condorcet was a friend of almost all the distinguished men of his time and enthusiastic toward the progressive views then current among French men of letters. A protégé of the French philosopher and mathematician Jean Le Rond d'Alembert, he took an active part in the preparation of the *Encyclopédie*. He was elected to the permanent secretary-ship of the Academy of Sciences in 1777 and to the French Academy in 1782 and was a member of other European academies. In 1785 he published his *Essai sur l'application de l'analyse à la probabilité des décisions rendues à la pluralité des voix* (*Essay on the Application of Analysis to the Probability of Majority Decisions*), a remarkable work that has a distinguished place in the history of the rules of probability. A second edition, greatly enlarged and completely recast, appeared in 1805 under the title of *Éléments du calcul des probabilités et son application aux jeux de hasard, à la loterie et aux jugements des hommes*.

In 1786 he married Sophie de Grouchy (1764–1822), who was said to have been one of the most beautiful women of her time. Her salon at the Hôtel des Monnaies, where Condorcet lived in his capacity as inspector general of the mint, was quite famous.

Condorcet published his *Vie de M. Turgot* in 1786 and his *Vie de Voltaire* in 1789. Both works were widely and eagerly read and are perhaps, from a purely literary point of view, the best of Condorcet's writings.

The outbreak of the French Revolution, which he greeted with enthusiasm, involved him in a great deal of political activity. He was elected to represent Paris in the Legislative Assembly and became its secretary, was active in the reform of the educational system, was chief author of the address to the European powers in 1791, and in 1792 he presented a scheme for a system of state education, which was the basis of that ultimately adopted.

Condorcet was one of the first to declare for a republic, and in August 1792 he drew up the declaration justifying the suspension of the king and the summoning of the National Convention. In the convention he represented the département of Aisne and was a member of the committee on the constitution. His draft of a new constitution, representative of the Girondins, the more moderate political group during the Revolution, was rejected, however, in favour of that of the Jacobins, a more radical political group whose dominating figure was Robespierre. In the trial of Louis XVI he voted against the death penalty. But his independent attitude became dangerous in the wake of the Revolution when Robespierre's radical measures triumphed, and his opposition to the arrest of the Girondins led to his being outlawed.

To occupy his mind while he was in hiding, some of his friends prevailed on him to engage in the work by which he is best known, the *Esquisse d'un tableau historique des progrès de l'esprit humain* (1795; *Sketch for a Historical Picture of the Progress of the Human Mind*). Its fundamental idea is that of the continuous progress of the human race to an ultimate perfection. The stages that the human race has already gone through, or, in other words, the great epochs of history, are regarded as nine in number. There is an epoch of the future—a 10th epoch—and the most original part of Condorcet's treatise is that which is devoted to it.

While Condorcet was under proscription as a Girondin, some of the other works he wrote were published by friends and others were issued after his death. Still interested in public affairs and believing that the house in which he had been hiding was watched, he escaped and, after hiding in thickets and quarries for three days, entered the village of Clamart on the evening of March 27, 1794. His appearance betrayed him, and he was taken to Bourg-la-Reine and imprisoned. On the morning of March 29 he was found dead; whether from exhaustion or poisoning is unknown.

Wholly a man of the Enlightenment, an advocate of economic freedom, religious toleration, legal and educational reform, equal rights for women—including women's suffrage—and the abolition of slavery, Condorcet sought to extend the empire of reason to social affairs. Rather than elucidate human behavior, as had been done thus far, by recourse to either the moral or physical sciences, he sought to explain it by a merger of the two sciences that eventually became transmuted into the discipline of sociology.

CONFUCIUS

(b. 551–d. 479 BCE)

For more than 2,000 years the Chinese people were guided by the ideals of Confucianism. Its founder and greatest teacher was Confucius, whose humane philosophy also influenced the civilization of all of eastern Asia.

Many legends were spread to describe Confucius's beliefs. According to one story, he and his disciples passed a cemetery where a woman was weeping at a graveside. She told them she was crying because "My husband's father was killed here by a tiger, then my husband, and now my son has met the same fate." When they asked her why she did not leave such a fatal spot, she answered that in this place there was no oppressive government. "Remember this, my children," said Confucius, "oppressive government is fiercer and more feared than a tiger."

Confucius always said of himself that he was a "transmitter, not a maker." He collected and edited the poetry, music, and historical writings of what he considered the golden age.

Confucius never claimed to be more than a man. Yet when he died he was revered almost as a god. Temples were erected in his honor in every city of China. His grave at Qufu, in what is now Shandong Province, became a place of pilgrimage.

Although Confucianism is commonly called a religion in the West, it is rather a system of moral conduct. Confucius did not talk of God but of goodness. He did not teach about any God, saying simply, "Respect the

A statue of Confucius, watching over a temple in Beijing, China. Pan Hong/Flickr/Getty Images

gods, but have as little to do with them as possible." His attention was centered on making people better in their lifetime, and his *Analects* are wise sayings.

Confucius is the Latinized form of the philosopher's Chinese name, which was Kongfuzi or Kongzi, meaning "Master Kong." He was born as Kongqiu in a poor but noble family. His father died when the boy was three years old. When he was only six, people noted his fondness for setting out sacrifices and for ceremony. After his marriage at age 19, he worked for the governor of his district, first as a keeper of stores and then as an overseer of parks and livestock. At the age of 22 he began his lifework as a teacher by establishing a school. He accepted valuable aid from some of his students, but he also welcomed students who could afford to pay only a small fee.

After some years of teaching and travel, he settled in Shandong for 15 years. When he was 52 years old, he was rewarded with an appointment as governor of a province. He performed his task so well that a neighboring governor became jealous and plotted his overthrow. Confucius then went into voluntary exile and wandered about for 13 years. Discouraged, he returned to his native state of Lu in his 69th year and died three years later. He had one son and two daughters. In spite of the communist revolution, his teachings have had a great effect on Chinese history and culture.

BENEDETTO CROCE

(b. 1866–d. 1952)

Benedetto Croce was born on Feb. 25, 1866, in Pescasseroli, Italy, but he spent most of his life in Naples. An eloquent historian, philosopher, and humanist in the early 20th century, Croce was also a noted patriot of Italy. During the regime of Italian dictator Benito Mussolini, Croce became the symbol of the opposition to fascism.

He found university life uninspiring, so he dropped out and went on to become an entirely self-taught scholar. In the course of his studies he developed definite ideas on how a free democratic society should be structured. In 1903 he founded *La Critica*, a journal of social and cultural criticism. For the next 41 years he not only published his own works in it but also reviewed significant literary, philosophical, and historical works from all over Europe. Through this journal he became an influential molder of public opinion.

Croce became a senator in 1910 and served as the minister of education from 1920 until 1921, at which time he was dismissed for opposing Mussolini's regime. After Mussolini's defeat in the mid-1940s Croce refounded the suppressed Liberal party and worked to restore Italy to the ideals in which he believed. The postwar democratic Italy was greatly inspired by his authority and spirit. In 1947 he retired from government work to found the Italian Institute for Historical Studies in Naples.

He continued writing and publishing until his death in Naples on Nov. 20, 1952. His most significant works were the four-volume *Filosofia dello spirito* (1902–17; *Philosophy of the Spirit*) and *La storia come pensiero e come azione* (1938; *History as the Story of Liberty*).

DEMOCRITUS

(b. 460? BCE–d. 370? BCE)

The first known theory of atomism—that matter is composed of elementary particles that are minute and indivisible—was originated by the ancient Greek philosopher Leucippus. His pupil Democritus substantially developed and systematized this theory. In some ways, his work predicted the findings of physicists more than 2,000 years later.

Very little is known for certain about Democritus' life. According to tradition, he was a well-to-do citizen of Abdera, in Thrace, who traveled extensively in the East. He is said to have lived a long life.

Democritus believed that the universe is composed of both the Being (the physical world) and the Void (empty space). The Being, he theorized, is made up of an infinite number of absolutely small particles that cannot be broken apart or otherwise altered. He named these particles atomos, which means "indivisible." All matter, he believed, is composed of these same basic "atoms," which are essentially identical. The different qualities that humans perceive in matter, such as temperature, taste, shape, texture, and color, result from impressions created by variations in the size, shape, and arrangement of the fundamental atoms.

The atoms described by Democritus are not the same particles, however, as the atoms of contemporary science. When British chemist John Dalton began developing modern atomic theory in the early 19th century, he applied the ancient Greek name atom to the particle he identified as the basic building block of matter, in honor of Democritus.

Democritus also developed an ethical system and is believed to have written on astronomy, mathematics, literature, and language. He is said to have written 73 works, but only fragments, mainly of his works on ethics, have survived.

JACQUES DERRIDA

(b. 1930–d. 2004)

D errida was born on July 15, 1930, in El Biar, Alg. Derrida is best known for developing deconstruction, a form of philosophical and literary analysis. This approach involves, in part, closely examining the language and logic of a written work, revealing its underlying assumptions, and showing how contradictions within the text itself weaken those assumptions. Derrida challenged the basic oppositions in texts of Western philosophy between pairs of concepts—such as mind and body or nature and culture—in which one is taken to be fundamental and the other secondary. In many of his essays and books, for example, he critically examined texts in which speech was assumed to be a more authentic form of language than writing. He argued that this opposition of speech and writing is neither natural nor necessary.

In 1949 he moved to Paris, France, where he received an advanced degree in philosophy from the École Normale Supérieure in 1956. For many years he taught philosophy in Paris: at the Sorbonne (1960–64), the École Normale Supérieure (1964–84), and the École des Hautes Études en Sciences

Jacques Derrida, photographed in Paris in the 1980s. Raphael Gaillarde/ Gamma-Rapho/Getty Images

Sociales (1984–99). In later years Derrida also lectured worldwide and taught at several universities, including the University of California at Irvine.

Beginning in the 1960s, Derrida wrote numerous works on the nature of language and meaning that were both highly influential and controversial. In *L'Écriture et la différence* (*Writing and Difference*), *De la grammatologie* (*Of Grammatology*), and *La Voix et le phénomène* (*Speech and Phenomena*), all published in 1967, and in *Marges de la philosophie* (*Margins of Philosophy*), published in 1972, he evaluated the representation of writing and speech in major works in the history of Western thought. Some of his later writings explored psychoanalysis, literary criticism, aesthetic theory, justice and the law, and friendship and politics. He died on Oct. 8, 2004, in Paris.

RENÉ DESCARTES

(b. 1596–d. 1650)

René Descartes was born on March 31, 1596, at La Haye (now Descartes), in the Touraine region of France. Both modern philosophy and modern mathematics began with the work of Descartes. His invention of coordinate geometry prepared the way for further advances in mathematics. He also insisted that knowledge in the sciences should be based not on probabilities but on certainties derived from observations and experiments.

At the renowned Jesuit school of La Flèche, he was taught philosophy, the humanities, science, mathematics, and the arts. After getting a law degree at the University of Poitiers in 1616, he traveled and served as a volunteer in Dutch and Bavarian armies to broaden his experience.

In 1619 Descartes developed coordinate geometry, in which points are represented as pairs of numbers and lines and curves are represented as algebraic equations. This allows geometric problems to be solved with algebra. In that same year, he concluded that the universe has a mathematically logical structure and that a single method of reasoning,

Portrait believed to be of the French philosopher and mathematician René Descartes. DEA/G. Dagli Orti/De Agostini/ Getty Images

based on mathematics, could apply to all natural sciences. Descartes recommended breaking down a problem into its simplest parts, systematically deducing one conclusion from another, moving from simple to complex, and finally rechecking the reasoning.

With religious intolerance mounting in France, in 1628 Descartes moved to Holland, a tolerant society in which he was freer to pursue new ways of thinking without being persecuted as a heretic. He lived and worked in seclusion in various parts of the country for some 20 years.

While in Holland, Descartes attempted to discover a first principle, on which to build philosophical knowledge. To do this, he rejected all types of knowledge about which he could possibly be deceived, including knowledge obtained through the senses, through reasoning, or based on authority, or experts. He determined that he could not doubt the statement "I think, therefore I am," and thus his first principle was established.

Descartes developed a proof that both God and the material world exist. He believed that the world is made up of two fundamentally different substances, mind and matter. The mind, he argued, is immortal because it does not occupy space and cannot be broken apart. Descartes believed that a mind has will and intelligence, while matter—including the human body—operates by mechanical principles like a machine.

Descartes's work brought him both fame and controversy. His major writings on methodology and philosophy were *Discours de la méthode* (*Discourse on Method*, 1637) and *Meditationes de Prima Philosophia* (*Meditations on First Philosophy*, 1641). His application of algebra to geometry appeared as an essay accompanying his *Discourse*. He also published works about morals, medicine, and physics.

In 1649 Descartes was invited to join the court of the queen of Sweden. Unused to the climate, he became ill and died in Stockholm, Swed., on Feb. 11, 1650.

JOHN DEWEY
(b. 1859–d. 1952)

John Dewey was born in Burlington, Vt., on Oct. 20, 1859. He attended the University of Vermont and Johns Hopkins University. One of the most notable American philosophers of the 20th century, John Dewey was also a pioneer in educational theory and method. Out of his ideas developed the progressive education movement that was very influential in schools until about 1950. In philosophy he shares with William James and Charles Sanders Peirce the distinction of founding the movement called pragmatism.

In 1884 he went to the University of Michigan as an instructor in philosophy and psychology. From 1894 to 1904 he headed a department of philosophy, psychology, and education at the University of Chicago. In 1904 Dewey moved to Columbia University in New York City as professor of philosophy. He remained there for the rest of his teaching career.

Dewey and his wife, the former Alice Chipman, started the Laboratory School at the University of Chicago to test his educational theories. Learning by doing was the heart of his method. The children were given freedom to learn in accordance with their needs and experiences. The faculty was able to study child behavior, a new area of study at the time.

Dewey regarded the school as a community—a part of society. He looked upon education as a process of living, not as preparation for later living. His ideas were incorporated in a number of books, including the influential *The School and Society*, published in 1899, and *Experience and Education* (1938). In philosophy, Dewey's pragmatic theories insisted that the way to test ideas was to check them against their consequences rather than to claim their agreement with supposedly self-evident truth. His philosophy was suited to American life, characterized by its respect for science and technology, its diversity, and its practicality. When faced with a problem, said Dewey, a person must logically examine the options open to him to find the best solution supported by the facts. This method of inquiry and testing should be applied to moral and social questions, as well as to technological and scientific ones. His theories were set forth in a number of books, including *Reconstruction in Philosophy* (1920), *Experience and Nature* (1925), *Art as Experience* (1934), and *Freedom and Culture* (1939). Dewey retired from teaching in 1930. He died in New York City on June 1, 1952.

WILHELM DILTHEY

(b. 1833–d. 1911)

Wilhelm Dithley was born on Nov. 19, 1833, at Biebrich, near Wiesbaden, Nassau. He was a German philosopher who made important contributions to a methodology of the humanities and other human sciences.

Dilthey was the son of a Reformed Church theologian. After he finished grammar school in Wiesbaden, he began to study theology, first at Heidelberg, then at Berlin, where he soon transferred to philosophy. After completing exams in theology and philosophy, he taught for some time at secondary schools in Berlin but soon abandoned this to dedicate himself to scholarly endeavors. During these years he was bursting with energy, and his investigations led him into diverse directions. Hundreds of reviews and essays testify to an almost inexhaustible productivity.

In 1864 he took his doctorate at Berlin and obtained the right to lecture. He was appointed to a chair at the University of Basel in 1866; appointments to Kiel, in 1868, and Breslau, in 1871, followed. In 1882 he succeeded R.H. Lotze at the University of Berlin, where he spent the remainder of his life.

During these years Dilthey led the quiet life of a scholar, devoid of great external excitement and in total dedication to his work. He searched for the philosophical foundation of what he first and rather vaguely summarized as the "sciences of man, of society, and the state," which he later called *Geisteswissenschaften* ("human sciences")—a term that eventually gained general recognition to collectively denote the fields of history, philosophy, religion, psychology, art, literature, law, politics, and economics. In 1883, as a result of these studies, the first volume of his *Einleitung in die Geisteswissenschaften* (*Introduction to Human Sciences*) appeared. The second volume, on which he worked continually, never did appear. This introductory work yielded a series of important essays; one of these—his "Ideen über eine beschreibende und zergliedernde Psychologie" (1894; "Ideas Concerning a Descriptive and Analytical Psychology")—instigated the formation of a cognitive (*Verstehen*), or structural, psychology. During the last years of his life, Dilthey resumed this work on a new level in his treatise *Der Aufbau der geschichtlichen Welt in den Geisteswissenschaften* (1910; "The Structure of the Historical World in the Human Sciences"), which was also left unfinished.

Opposed to the trend in the historical and social sciences to approximate the methodological ideal of the natural sciences, Dilthey tried to establish the humanities as interpretative sciences in their own right. Dilthey emphasized that the essence of human beings cannot be grasped by introspection but only from knowledge of all of history; this understanding, however, can never be final because history itself never is: "The prototype 'man' disintegrates during the process of history." For this reason, his philosophical works were closely connected to his historical studies. From these works later arose the encompassing scheme of his *Studien zur Geschichte des deutschen Geistes* ("Studies Concerning the History of the German Mind"); the notes for this work make up a complete coherent manuscript, but only parts have been published.

Dilthey held that historical consciousness—i.e., the consciousness of the historical relativity of all ideas, attitudes, and institutions—is the most characteristic and challenging fact in the intellectual life of the modern world. Dilthey was suspicious of rationally constructed systems and preferred to leave questions unsettled, realizing that they involved complexity. For a long time, therefore, he was regarded primarily as a sensitive cultural historian who lacked the power of systematic thought. Only posthumously, through the editorial and interpretative work of his disciples, did the significance of the methodology of his historical philosophy of life emerge.

EPICTETUS

(b. 60 – d. circa 135 CE)

In his youth the Greek Stoic philosopher Epictetus was a slave. His real name is unknown. "Epictetus" means "acquired. " He was born in Phrygia in about CE 60, and when he was a boy he became the property of (was acquired by) a Roman. In Rome the slave managed to attend lectures on philosophy. After he won freedom, he became a teacher.

In about CE 90 Emperor Domitian forced all philosophers out of Italy. Epictetus went to Nicopolis, in Epirus, where he taught the doctrines of Stoicism. His teachings were based on freedom of the will, trust in providence, and obedience to conscience. His philosophy was preserved by Arrian, one of his pupils, in *Discourses* and *Handbook*.

EPICURUS

(b. 341 BCE–d. 270 BCE)

Freedom from pain in the body and from trouble in the mind is the goal of a happy life. This was the teaching of the Greek philosopher Epicurus, who lived from 341 to 270 BCE. To many people Epicureanism has often meant a simple devotion to pleasure, comfort, and high living with little thought for the consequences. But the ideas of Epicurus were far more complex. In his lifetime, and for centuries afterward, he was considered a moral reformer.

The ideas of Epicurus on how a person should live were based on his understanding of the natural world and his beliefs about the human body-soul relationship. Like Democritus before him, Epicurus believed that the universe is made up of material bodies and space, or the void. Bodies are composed of individual elements called atoms. The universe is unlimited, and so is the number of atoms. Atoms are of different shapes, and the number of atoms of each shape is infinite.

Both the human body and soul are composed of atoms. The atoms of the soul are thin and distributed throughout the body. It is the soul that is responsible for all sense perception. Sensation is the sole source of knowledge, as all sense perceptions are true—whether of seeing, hearing, touching, smelling, or tasting. Error may arise, however, if the mind forms a wrong opinion about what the senses perceive. As long as the soul is protected by the body, it is capable of communicating sensations to it. When it leaves the body it is scattered and lost, and the body is no longer able to feel anything.

If sensations are the basis of knowledge, the purpose of knowledge is to avoid those sensations that cause pain and to seek out those that give pleasure both to body and mind. While every pleasure is in itself good, not every pleasure is to be pursued because some pleasures may mean painful consequences or annoyances that outweigh the pleasures themselves. This means that the individual must learn to choose between pleasures that are really good and those that only seem to be good.

To live well requires the exercise of practical wisdom—moderation, justice, and courage—to balance pleasures against pains and to accept when necessary those pains that lead to greater pleasures. Thus Epicureanism is not just a self-serving attitude. It may be necessary, for example, to engage in battle in order to achieve the greater goal of peace. It is necessary to treat other people with justice because it is painful to be treated unjustly. Epicurus recommended the cultivation of friendship as both useful and desirable. He also claimed that the pleasures of the mind are more enduring than those of the body.

AL-FARABI

(b. circa 878–d. circa 950)

Al-Farabi, in full Muḥammad ibn Muḥammad ibn Ṭarkhān ibn Awzalagh (or Uzlugh) al-Fārābī, was born circa 878, in Turkistan.

39

He was a Muslim philosopher, one of the outstanding thinkers of medieval Islam. He was regarded in the medieval Islamic world as the greatest philosophical authority after Aristotle.

Very little is known of al-Farabi's life, and his ethnic origin is a matter of dispute. He eventually moved from Central Asia to Baghdad, where most of his works were written. Al-Farabi was not a member of the court society, and neither did he work in the administration of the central government. In 942 he took up residence at the court of the prince Sayf al-Dawlah, where he remained, mostly in Ḥalab (modern Aleppo, Syria), until the time of his death.

Al-Farabi's philosophical thinking was nourished in the heritage of the Arabic Aristotelian teachings of 10th-century Baghdad. His great service to Islam was to take the Greek heritage, as it had become known to the Arabs, and show how it could be used to answer questions with which Muslims were struggling. To Al-Farabi, philosophy had come to an end in other parts of the world but had a chance for new life in Islam. Islam as a religion, however, was of itself not sufficient for the needs of a philosopher. He saw human reason as being superior to revelation. Religion provided truth in a symbolic form to non-philosophers, who were not able to understand it in its purer forms. The biggest chunk of his work was directed to the problem of the correct ordering of the state. Just as God rules the universe, so should the philosopher, as the most perfect kind of man, rule the state.

He thus related the political upheavals of his time to the separation of the philosopher from government. Al-Farabi died in Damascus in circa 950.

MICHEL FOUCAULT

(b. 1926–d. 1984)

French structuralist philosopher Michel Foucault was born in Poitiers. He studied in Paris under Marxist philosopher Louis Althusser and later taught at the University of Clermont-Ferrand from

1960 to 1968 and the Collège de France from 1970 to 1984. His early work concerned the history of mental illness and society's response to it. *Madness and Civilization* (1961) is a study of society's use of the concept of madness in the 17th century.

Discipline and Punish: The Birth of the Prison (1975) is an examination of the origins of the modern penal system. His books argue that asylums and prisons are society's devices for exclusion and that by surveying social attitudes toward these institutions, one can examine the development and uses of power.

Michel Foucault in an undated photograph, probably from the 1980s. AFP/ Getty Images

GOTTLOB FREGE

(b. 1848–d. 1925)

F riedrich Ludwig Gottlob Frege was born on Nov. 8, 1848, in Wismar, Mecklenburg-Schwerin. In 1869 Frege entered the University of Jena, where he studied for two years. For two more years he studied mathematics, physics, chemistry, and philosophy at the University of Göttingen. He spent his entire working life as a teacher at Jena, lecturing in all branches of mathematics.

In 1879 Frege published his *Conceptual Notation*, in which, for the first time, a system of mathematical logic in the modern sense was presented. There followed a period of intensive work on the philosophy of logic and mathematics, which resulted in *The Foundations of Arithmetic* (1884), a masterpiece of philosophical writing.

In 1902, however, some errors were pointed out in his system of logic by the philosopher Bertrand Russell. This effectively marked the end of his productive life. He retired during World War I and went to live in Bad Kleinen, in Mecklenburg, where he died on July 26, 1925. Recognition of his importance was delayed until long after his death.

AL-GHAZALI

(b. 1058–d. 1111)

One of the most prominent figures in the history of the religion of Islam was a jurist, theologian, and mystic named al-Ghazali. One of his more significant contributions to thought was bringing Greek philosophical concepts and methods into the mainstream of Islam.

Abu Hamid Muhammad Al-Ghazali was born at Tus in eastern Iran in 1058. He was educated there and at Jorjan and Nishapur. In 1085 he was invited to go to the court of the Seljuq sultan at Baghdad, where he became chief professor at the Nizamiyah College. In 1095 al-Ghazali abandoned his post, disposed of his wealth, and adopted the life of a poor mystic seeker after truth. He settled at Tus, where his followers joined him to form a monastic community. In 1106 he returned to teaching, at Nishapur, convinced that he was a "renewer" of Islam who was to appear at the start of a century. (The year 1106 was 500 in the Muslim calendar.) He remained there until 1110, when he returned to Tus.

More than 400 works are credited to al-Ghazali, but it is likely that no more than 50 of them are his. The most significant was *The Revival of the Religious Sciences*. In 40 chapters he explained how the teachings and practices of Islam could be made the basis of a devotional life, leading to higher stages of mysticism. In *The Deliverer from Error* he defended his abandoning of a teaching career in favor of a mystic life.

His philosophical studies culminated in *The Inconsistency—or Incoherence—of the Philosophers*, in which he defended Islam against such thinkers as Avicenna, many of whose views were contrary to the accepted doctrines of Islam. His earlier book *The Aims of the Philosophers* was translated into Latin and was widely read in Europe. He also wrote on legal principles, Christianity, and the sect of Assassins. He died in Tus on Dec. 18, 1111.

JÜRGEN HABERMAS

(b. 1929–d.)

Jürgen Habermas was born on June 18, 1929, in Düsseldorf, Ger. Habermas is considered to be the most important German philosopher of the second half of the 20th century. A highly influential social and political thinker, Habermas was generally identified with the critical social theory developed from the 1920s by the Institute for Social Research in Frankfurt am Main, Ger., also known as the Frankfurt School. He belonged to the second generation of the Frankfurt Institute, following first-generation and founding figures such as Max Horkheimer, Theodor Adorno, and Herbert Marcuse. His work powerfully influenced many disciplines, including communication studies, cultural studies, moral theory, law, linguistics, literary theory, and philosophy.

Habermas grew up in Gummersbach, Ger. At age 10 he joined the Hitler Youth, as did many of his contemporaries, and at age 15, during the last months of World War II, he was sent to the Western Front. After the Nazi defeat in May 1945, he completed his secondary education and attended the Universities of Bonn, Göttingen, and Zürich. At Bonn he received a Ph.D. in philosophy in 1954 with a dissertation on Friedrich Schelling. From 1956 to 1959 he worked as Theodor Adorno's first assistant at the Institute for Social Research. Habermas left the institute in 1959 and completed his second doctorate (his habilitation thesis, which qualified him to teach at the university level) in 1961 under the political scientist Wolfgang Abendroth at the University of Marburg. His thesis was published with additions in 1962 as *Strukturwandel der Öffentlichkeit (The Structural Transformation of the Public Sphere)*. In 1961 Habermas became a privatdozent (unsalaried professor and lecturer) in Marburg, and in 1962 he was named extraordinary professor (professor without chair) at the University of Heidelberg. He succeeded Max Horkheimer as professor of philosophy and sociology at the Johann Wolfgang Goethe University of Frankfurt am Main (Frankfurt University) in 1964. After 10 years as director of the Max Planck Institute in Starnberg (1971–81), he returned to Frankfurt, where he retired in 1994. Thereafter he taught in the United States at Northwestern University (Evanston, Ill.) and New York University and lectured worldwide.

In *The Structural Transformation of the Public Sphere*, Habermas showed how modern European salons, cafés, and literary groups contain the resources for democratizing the public sphere. In his 1965 inaugural lecture at Frankfurt University, *Erkenntnis und Interesse* (1965; *Knowledge and Human Interests*), and in the book of the same title published three years later, Habermas set forth the foundations of a normative version of critical social theory, the Marxist social theory developed by Horkheimer, Adorno, and other members of the Frankfurt Institute from the 1920s onward. Habermas took a linguistic-communicative turn in *Theorie des kommunikativen Handelns* (1981; *The Theory of Communicative Action*). He argued that human interaction in one of its fundamental forms is "communicative" rather than "strategic" in nature, insofar as it is aimed at mutual understanding and agreement rather than at the achievement of the self-interested goals of individuals.

Habermas's findings carried wide-ranging normative implications. In *Moralbewusstsein und kommunikatives Handeln* (1983; *Moral Consciousness and Communicative Action*), he elaborated a general theory of "discourse ethics," or "communicative ethics," which concerns the ethical presuppositions of ideal communication that would have to be invoked in an ideal communication community. In a series of lectures published as *Philosophische Diskurs der Moderne* (1985; *The Philosophical Discourse of Modernity*), Habermas defended from postmodern criticism the Enlightenment ideal of normative rationality and specifically the ideal that unconstrained communication is guided by reasons that can be rejected or redeemed by speakers and hearers as true, right, or sincere.

Habermas was criticized by both the postmodern left and the neo-conservative right for his trust in the power of rational discussion to resolve major domestic and international conflicts. Habermas responded to critics at both ends of the political spectrum by developing a more robust communicative theory of democracy, law, and constitutions in *Faktizität und Geltung* (1992; *Between Facts and Norms*), *Die Einbeziehung des Anderen* (1996; *The Inclusion of the Other*), and *Die postnationale Konstellation* (1998; *The Postnational Constitution*). In *Zeit der Übergänge* (2001; *Time of Transitions*), he offered global democratic alternatives to wars that employ terrorism as well as to the "war on terrorism."

From the postwar years onward, Habermas engaged with a variety of thinkers who were preoccupied with the theme of hope against hope: existentialists such as Søren Kierkegaard and Jean-Paul Sartre, Christian political theologians such as Johann Baptist Metz and Jürgen Moltmann, and Jewish thinkers Walter Benjamin, Hans Jonas, and Herbert Marcuse. Habermas returned to such issues in the early 21st century in *Die Zukunft der menschlichen Natur* (2001; *The Future of Human Nature*); *Glauben und Wissen* (2001; "Faith and Knowledge"), *Religion and Rationality: Essays on Reason, God, and Modernity* (2002), and other works.

GEORG WILHELM FRIEDRICH HEGEL
(b. 1770–d. 1831)

Georg Wilhelm Friedrich Hegel was born in Stuttgart, Ger., on Aug. 27, 1770. One of the most influential of the 19th-century German philosophers, Georg Wilhelm Friedrich Hegel also wrote on psychology, law, history, art, and religion. Karl Marx based his philosophy of history on Hegel's law of thought, called the dialectic. In this dialectic, an idea, or thesis, contains within itself an opposing idea, called antithesis. Out of the inevitable conflict between these opposing concepts is born a third, totally new thought, the synthesis. Applied to history by the Marxists, Hegel's concepts were used to formulate the notion of the class struggle. From the conflict over the ownership of the means of production would arise a new classless society—the synthesis.

Søren Kierkegaard's rejection of Hegelianism influenced the development of existentialism.

Hegel's father was a government official. Hegel went to Tübingen in 1788, where he studied philosophy and theology. After graduating he supported himself by tutoring until 1801, when he began to lecture at the University of Jena. Forced to leave because of the Napoleonic wars, he became the principal of a gymnasium (high school) in Nuremberg. There he married Marie von Tucher. The older of Hegel's two sons, Karl, became an eminent historian.

At Nuremberg Hegel worked on his *Science of Logic*, which was published between 1812 and 1816. The success of this work brought him three offers of professorships. He taught at Heidelberg for a time and then in 1818 went to the University of Berlin. Students came from all parts of Europe to study with him. He became rector of the university in 1830. He died of cholera in Berlin on November 14, 1831.

The significance of Hegel's ideas stems in part from the fact that they can be applied not only to abstract thought but also to psychology, religion, and history. An essential element of his system was his belief that reality can only be understood when viewed as a whole and that any attempt to discover truth by scrutinizing a single facet of reality is doomed to failure.

MARTIN HEIDEGGER

(b. 1889–d. 1976)

Martin Heidegger was born in Messkirch, Ger., on Sept. 26, 1889. The work of Heidegger changed the course of 20th-century philosophy in continental Europe. He was a student of Edmund Husserl, the founder of phenomenology, a philosophical discipline concerned with describing as directly and exactly as possible the contents of conscious experience. Heidegger was also a phenomenologist, but he studied the nature of "being," or existence, and specifically the nature of the "human" being—the kind of being that human beings have. The question "What is the meaning of being?" is central to his masterpiece, *Being and Time* (1927). This work is notoriously difficult to read. Nevertheless, it was a strong influence on Jean-Paul Sartre and other existentialists. Heidegger's work has also been highly influential in other fields of the humanities, especially literary criticism, psychology, and theology.

As a young man Heidigger joined the Jesuits as a novice. He studied theology and later philosophy at the University of Freiburg. He taught there from 1915 until 1945 except for a five-year period at the University of Marburg (1923–28). When the Nazis came to power in 1933, he joined the Nazi party and supported their policies. For this reason, after World War II ended he was banned from teaching. The ban was lifted in 1950, however, and he resumed lecturing. He died in Messkirch on May 26, 1976.

In his work, Heidegger challenged the assumptions of Husserl and other phenomenologists, who conceived of the being of things as limited to their status as phenomena within the consciousness of the individual. Instead, Heidegger regarded the being of things as consisting primarily of the ways in which they are used and manipulated by individuals in their daily lives. Likewise, the being of the individual consists primarily of the ways in which he encounters and interacts with things, not in his conscious experience of things as a detached and isolated subject. Because of this, Heidegger called the being of the individual "being-in-the-world," or (in German) *Dasein*.

The influence of Martin Heidegger has been felt across many disciplines in addition to philosophy. Apic/Hulton Archive/Getty Images

CARL GUSTAV HEMPEL

(b. 1905–d. 1997)

Carl Gustav Hempel was born on Jan. 8, 1905, Oranienburg, Ger. The German-born American philosopher was formerly a member of the Berlin school of logical positivism, a group that viewed logical and mathematical statements as revealing only the basic structure of language, but not essentially descriptive of the physical world.

Hempel attended several universities, including the University of Berlin (Ph.D. , 1934), where he studied philosophy with Hans Reichenbach. With the growth of the Nazi power in Germany, Hempel emigrated to the United States in the late 1930s. He taught at Yale and Princeton universities and the University of Pittsburgh. While probing the nature of theoretical science, Hempel advanced the precision of sociological concepts. His English writings include *Fundamentals of Concept Formation in Empirical Science* (1952) and *Philosophy of Natural Science* (1966). He died on Nov. 9, 1997, in Princeton Township, N.J., U.S.A.

HERACLEITUS

(b. 540 BCE–d. 480 BCE)

Heracleitus, also spelled Heraclitus was born in c. 540 BCE, Ephesus, in Anatolia, now Selçuk, Tur. He was a Greek philosopher remembered for his cosmology, in which fire forms the basic material principle of an orderly universe. Little is known about his life, and the one book he apparently wrote is lost. His views survive in the short fragments quoted and attributed to him by later authors.

Though he was primarily concerned with explanations of the world around him, Heracleitus also stressed the need for people to live together in social harmony. He complained that most people failed to comprehend the logos (Greek: "reason"), the universal principle through which all things are interrelated and all natural events occur, and thus lived like dreamers with a false view of the world. A significant manifestation of thelogos, Heracleitus claimed, is the underlying connection between opposites. For example, health and disease define each other. Good and evil, hot and cold, and other opposites are similarly related. In addition, he noted that a single substance may be perceived in varied ways—seawater is both harmful (for human beings) and beneficial (for fishes). His understanding of the relation of opposites to each other enabled him to overcome the chaotic and divergent nature of the world, and he asserted that the world exists as a coherent system in which a change in one direction is ultimately balanced by a corresponding change in another. Between all things there is a hidden connection, so that those that are apparently "tending apart" are actually "being brought together."

Viewing fire as the essential material uniting all things, Heracleitus wrote that the world order is an "ever-living fire kindling in measures and being extinguished in measures." He extended the manifestations of fire to include not only fuel, flame, and smoke but also the ether in the upper atmosphere. Part of this air, or pure fire, "turns to" ocean, presumably as rain, and part of the ocean turns to earth. Simultaneously, equal masses of earth and sea everywhere are returning to the respective aspects of sea and fire. The resulting dynamic equilibrium maintains an orderly balance in the world. This persistence of unity despite change is illustrated by Heracleitus' famous analogy of life to a river: "Upon those who step into the same rivers different and ever different waters flow down." Plato later took this doctrine to mean that all things are in constant flux, regardless of how they appear to the senses.

Heracleitus was unpopular in his time and was frequently scorned by later biographers. His primary contribution lies in his apprehension of the formal unity of the world of experience.

THOMAS HOBBES

(b. 1588–d. 1679)

Thomas Hobbes was born in Westport in Wiltshire, Eng., on April 5, 1588. As a political theorist, Hobbes lived during the decades

Oil portrait of English philosopher Thomas Hobbes, by John Michael Wright. De Agostini/Getty Images

when absolute monarchy in Europe was drawing to a close and sentiments for popular democracy were emerging. In his book *Leviathan* (1651), he provided the formula for an ideal state in which all citizens would live together under terms of a social contract. To keep everyone from exercising too much freedom, however, there would be an absolute monarchy.

He graduated from Oxford University in 1608 and became a classical scholar and mathematician before taking an interest in the study of politics. His first work was a translation of Thucydides' *History of the Peloponnesian War* (1629). His fascination with mathematics began at age 40, when he read Euclid's *Elements*.

His study of geometry and physics led him to plan a three-volume work on the physical world, the human body, and citizenship. Returning to England in 1637 as events were progressing toward civil war, he wrote the third volume first under the title *The Elements of Law, Natural and Politic* (1640). The political crisis in England caused him to flee into exile in Paris, where he remained until 1651.

Hobbes enjoyed royal favor and security from his enemies beginning in 1660, when Charles II came to the throne. Hobbes had earlier tutored Charles in mathematics. He was briefly threatened with charges of heresy, but the king protected him. He continued writing and publishing almost up to the day of his death. He published a translation of Homer's *Odyssey* in 1675 and of the *Iliad* in 1676. Hobbes died in Derbyshire on Dec. 4, 1679.

DAVID HUME
(b. 1711–d. 1776)

A Scottish philosopher and historian, David Hume was a founder of the skeptical, or agnostic, school of philosophy. He had a significant influence on European intellectual life.

David Hume was born in Edinburgh, Scot., on April 26, 1711. His father, Joseph Hume (or Home), and his mother, Katherine Falconer, had grown up together as stepbrother and stepsister on the family estate of Ninewells in Berwickshire. Under the system of primogeniture Hume's older brother was heir to the estate.

David Hume was expected by his family to follow a traditional career in law. By the age of 18, however, after attending the University of Edinburgh from 1724 to 1726 and finding law unpleasant, he enthusiastically studied literature and philosophy.

From 1734 to 1737 Hume lived in France. There he wrote his first work, *A Treatise of Human Nature*. He was disappointed by its hostile reception and later dismissed it as an immature work that did not accurately reflect his views. In spite of this, the part on understanding continues to be widely read. Hume's more immediately successful Essays, *Moral and Political* was published in 1741–42 after he had returned to Ninewells.

For a while Hume worked as a tutor. In the late 1740s he served as secretary to General James St. Clair on military missions in Brittany, Vienna, and Turin. With the publication of *Political Discourses* in 1752, he began his rise to international fame.

In 1751 Hume had been appointed keeper of the library of the Faculty of Advocates in Edinburgh. Using its historical collection for his research, he wrote his spectacularly successful *A History of England*, published in four volumes between 1754 and 1761. For decades this history, or a shortened version of it, was used as a standard text in English schools.

Hume served for some years as secretary and then as chargé d'affaires in the British embassy in Paris. He returned to London in 1766 and worked for a while as undersecretary of state. In 1769 Hume retired to live with his sister. In 1775 he was stricken by an incurable intestinal cancer. He died in Edinburgh on Aug. 25, 1776.

Hume's philosophical writings cast doubt on the truth of church-supported dogmas. Not only did he deny miracles and other religious dogmas, but his theory of knowledge seemed to dent the reality of the world itself. He maintained that knowledge came from observation and experience. These, however, were just individual. A person's perceptions of objects were just that—perceptions.

In his political writings Hume held that government organization, though basically evil, is necessary to guarantee human happiness. In economic theory Hume argued that goods rather than money are the basis of wealth. He believed that each part of the world has special products or services to offer and was an early advocate of increased trade among the nations of the world. Despite the intellectual controversy he aroused, Hume was admired and loved by his many friends, which included members of the clergy. He never married but contented himself with securing the education of his brother's children.

EDMUND HUSSERL

(b. 1859–d. 1938)

Edmund Husserl was born on April 8, 1859, in Prossnitz, Moravia, Austrian Empire, now Prostějov, Czech Republic. He was a German philosopher, the founder of phenomenology, a method for the description and analysis of consciousness through which philosophy attempts to gain the character of a strict science.

Husserl was born into a Jewish family and completed his qualifying examinations in 1876 at the German public gymnasium in the neighboring city of Olmütz (Olomouc). He then studied physics, mathematics, astronomy, and philosophy at the universities of Leipzig, Berlin, and Vienna. In Vienna he received his doctor of philosophy degree in 1882 with a dissertation entitled *Beiträge zur Theorie der Variationsrechnung* ("Contributions to the Theory of the Calculus of Variations"). In the autumn of 1883, Husserl moved to Vienna to study with the philosopher and psychologist Franz Brentano and later married Malvine Steinschneider. She was his indispensable support until his death.

In 1887 Husserl qualified as a lecturer in the university (Habilitation). The title of his inaugural lecture in Halle was "Über die Ziele und Aufgaben der Metaphysik" ("On the Goals and Problems of Metaphysics.

Husserl then presented his ideas in the *Logische Untersuchungen* (1900–01; "Logical Investigations"), which employed a method of analysis that Husserl now designated as "phenomenological." The revolutionary significance of this work was only gradually recognized.

After the publication of the *Logische Untersuchungen*, Husserl was called, to the position of *ausserordentlicher Professor* (university lecturer) by the University of Göttingen.

The phenomenological analysis of experienced reality drew not only the German students but also many young foreign philosophers who came from the traditions of empiricism and pragmatism. Husserl gave each of his students the freedom to pursue suggestions in an independent way. He wanted his teaching to be not a transmission of finished results but rather the preparation for a responsible setting of the problem.

Husserl presented phenomenology's program and its systematic outline in the *Ideen zu einer reinen Phänomenologie und phänomenologischen Philosophie* (1913; *Ideas; General Introduction to Pure Phenomenology*), of which, however, only the first part was completed. (Completion of the second part was hindered by the outbreak of World War I.) With this work, Husserl wanted to give his students a manual. The result, however, was just the opposite and the phenomenological school fell apart.

In contrast to the esteem that Husserl enjoyed from his students, his position among his colleagues in Göttingen was always difficult. Thus his call in 1916 to the position of *ordentlicher Professor* (university professor) at the University of Freiburg meant a new beginning for Husserl in every respect. His inaugural lecture on "Die reine Phänomenologie, ihr Forschungsgebiet und ihre Methode" ("Pure Phenomenology, Its Area of Research and Its Method") circumscribed his program of work. He had understood World War I as the collapse of the old European world, in which spiritual culture, science, and philosophy had held an incontestable position.

In this sense he had set forth in his lectures on *Erste Philosophie* (1923–24; "First Philosophy") the thesis that phenomenology, with its method of reduction, is the way to the absolute vindication of life. Upon this basis, he continued his clarification of the relation between a psychological and a phenomenological analysis of consciousness and his research into the grounding of logic, which he published as the *Formale und transzendentale Logik: Versuch einer Kritik der logischen Vernunft* (1929; *Formal and Transcendental Logic*, 1969).

In 1919 the law faculty of the University of Bonn bestowed upon Husserl the title of *Dr. jur. honoris causa*. He was the first German scholar after the war to be invited to lecture at the University of London (1922). When he retired in 1928, Martin Heidegger became his successor. Only later did he see that Heidegger's chief work, *Sein und Zeit* (1927; *Being and Time*, 1962), had given phenomenology a turn that would lead down an entirely different path. Husserl's disappointment led to a cooling of their relationship after 1930.

Adolf Hitler's seizure of power in 1933 did not break Husserl's ability to work. Rather, the experience of this upheaval was, for him, the occasion for concentrating more than ever upon phenomenology's task of preserving the freedom of the mind. During this time, the Cercle Philosophique de Prague facilitated the classification and transcription of Husserl's unpublished manuscripts. Through the Cercle, Husserl received an invitation to address the German and Czechoslovakian University in Prague in the fall of 1935, after which many discussions took place in the smaller circles.

Out of these lectures came Husserl's last work, *Die Krisis der europäischen Wissenschaften und die transzendentale Phänomenologie: Eine Einleitung in die phänomenologische Philosophie* (1936; *The Crisis of European Sciences and Transcendental Phenomenology*, 1970), of which only the first part could appear, in a periodical for emigrants. The following period until the summer of 1937 was entirely devoted to the continuation of this work, in which Husserl developed for the first time his concept of the *Lebenswelt* ("life-world").

In the summer of 1937, the illness that made it impossible for him to continue his work set in. He died in April 1938, and his ashes were buried in the cemetery in Günterstal near Freiburg.

HYPATIA

(b. 355?CE–d. 415 CE)

A ncient Egyptian scholar Hypatia lived in Alexandria, Egypt, during the final years of the Roman Empire. She was the world's leading mathematician and astronomer of the time. She was also an important teacher of philosophy.

The year of Hypatia's birth is uncertain, though she may have been born about 355 CE. She was the daughter of Theon of Alexandria, a leading mathematician and astronomer who belonged to the Alexandrian Museum, a famous center of learning. Theon taught Hypatia mathematics, science, literature, philosophy, and art.

A wood engraving depicting the murder of Hypatia at the hands of a mob. Universal Images Group/Getty Images

Theon edited an important edition of Euclid's *Elements*, and he wrote commentaries on works by Ptolemy. Hypatia continued her father's program, which was essentially an effort to preserve the Greek mathematical and astronomical heritage during extremely difficult times. She wrote commentaries on works of geometry, number theory (an advanced branch of arithmetic), and astronomy. Unfortunately, none of her works has survived. Hypatia was also a popular teacher and lecturer on philosophy, attracting many loyal students and large audiences. She rose to become head of Alexandria's Neoplatonist school of philosophy, a school whose basic ideas derived from Plato.

Hypatia lived during a difficult time in Alexandria's history. The city was embroiled in a bitter religious conflict between Christians, Jews, and pagans (who believed in many gods). In 391 the Christian bishop of Alexandria had a pagan temple destroyed, even though it contained an important collection of classical literature that could not be replaced. Although Hypatia's teachings were not religious, some Christians saw them as pagan. Her views became less accepted in the city. In March 415 Hypatia was brutally murdered by a mob of Christian extremists. She became a powerful symbol of female learning and science and of scholarly pursuits in the face of ignorant prejudice.

IBN AL-'ARABI

(b. 1165–d. 1240)

Ibn al-Arabi, also called Al-Sheikh al-Akbar was born on July 28, 1165, in Murcia, Valencia. He was a celebrated Muslim mystic-philosopher who gave the mystical dimension of Islamic thought its first full-fledged philosophic expression. His major works are the monumental *Al-Futūḥāt al-Makkiyyah* ("The Meccan Revelations") and *Fuṣūṣ al-ḥikam* (1229; "The Bezels of Wisdom").

Ibn al-'Arabi was born in the southeast region of Spain. It was in Sevilla (Seville), then an outstanding center of Islamic culture and learning, that he received his early education. He stayed there for 30 years, studying traditional Islamic sciences. During those years he traveled a great deal and visited various cities of Spain and North Africa in search of masters of the Sufi (mystical) path who had achieved great spiritual progress and thus renown.

It was during one of these trips that Ibn al-Arabi had a dramatic encounter with Averroes in the city of Córdoba. Averroes, a close friend of the boy's father, had asked that the interview be arranged because he had heard of the extraordinary nature of the young, still beardless lad. After the early exchange of only a few words, it is said, the mystical depth of the boy so overwhelmed the old philosopher that he became pale and, dumbfounded, began trembling.

In 1198, while in Murcia, Ibn al-Arabi had a vision in which he felt he had been ordered to leave Spain and set out for the East. Thus began his pilgrimage to the Orient, from which he never was to return to his homeland. The first notable place he visited on this journey was Mecca (1201), where he "received a divine commandment" to begin his major work *Al-Futūh̬āt al-Makkiyyah*, which was to be completed much later in Damascus.

It was also in Mecca that Ibn al-Arabi became acquainted with a young girl of great beauty who, as a living embodiment of the eternal *sophia* (wisdom), was to play in his life a role much like that which Beatrice played for Dante. Her memories were eternalized by Ibn al-Arabi in a collection of love poems (*Tarjumān al-ashwāq*; "The Interpreter of Desires"), upon which he himself composed a mystical commentary.

After Mecca, Ibn al-Arabi visited Egypt (also in 1201) and then Anatolia, where, in Qonya, he met S̬adr al-Dīn al-Qūnawī, who was to become his most important follower and successor in the East. From Qonya he went on to Baghdad and Aleppo (modern H̬alab, Syria). By the time his long pilgrimage had come to an end at Damascus (1223), his fame had spread all over the Islamic world. Venerated as the greatest spiritual master, he spent the rest of his life in Damascus in peaceful contemplation, teaching, and writing. It was during his Damascus days that one of the most important works in mystical philosophy in Islam, *Fus̬ūs̬ al-h̬ikam*, was composed in 1229, about 10 years before his death. Consisting only of 27 chapters, the book is incomparably smaller than *Al-Futūh̬āt al-Makkiyyah*, but its importance as an expression of Ibn al-'Arabī's mystical thought in its most mature form cannot be overemphasized.

Ibn al'Arabi died in Damascus on November 16, 1240.

IBN GABIROL

(b. 1021?– d. 1058?)

Solomon ben Yehuda ibn Gabirol was born about 1021 in Málaga, Spain. A medieval Hebrew poet and philosopher, Ibn Gabirol wrote during the Spanish period. His Hebrew verse consists of both sacred and secular poems.

After a lonely childhood as a dependent orphan, he showed early promise as a poet and was soon recognized as a master of Hebrew. His secular poems reveal an intellectual mind that was sensitive to change. His sacred poems, which are meditative and devotional, humbly reflect the glory of God and longings for the release of suffering Jews. Many of the latter poems became part of the Hebrew liturgy, or worship, of the time. Among these is a mystical confessional called "Keter Malkhut" (Crown of the Kingdom), which expresses the grandeur of God as well as the insignificance of human struggling to master passion and desire. His secular poems include love odes, dirges, and praise of his friends.

Ibn Gabirol was also interested in philosophy. His major philosophical works were written in Arabic. Their translated titles are *The Improvement of the Moral Qualities* and *Fount of Life*. The latter had great influence on medieval scholars and was long believed to be written by a Christian. It was not until the 19th century that the scholar Salomon Munk proved the work to have been written by Ibn Gabirol. The Hebrew poet died around 1058 in Valencia.

WILLIAM JAMES

(b. 1842–d. 1910)

William James was born on Jan. 11, 1842, in New York City. He was an American philosopher and psychologist and had a remarkable variety of talents.

Most notably, James was a leader in the movement known as pragmatism, which stresses that the value of any idea or policy is based entirely on its usefulness and workability.

His early education, like that of his brother Henry, was varied. Although William's first ambition was to be an artist, he entered Harvard Medical School in 1864.

He was granted a degree in medicine in 1869, but by that time he had decided that he would not practice medicine. He had studied chemistry, comparative anatomy, and physiology. In 1865 he went on a geological expedition to Brazil with Louis Agassiz. James had also read widely in literature, history, and philosophy. He wrote literary criticism and became interested in psychology.

Outwardly a friendly, warm, and happy person, James was subject to periods of deep depression, partly because of constant ill health and partly because of his inability to find a suitable profession or philosophy. In 1870, however, he had an experience that gave him a sense of direction. He read Charles Renouvier's essays and gained a new insight into the power of free will as a moral force.

James was appointed an instructor in physiology at Harvard in 1872. He later taught psychology and philosophy and became famous as one of the outstanding teachers of his time.

In 1884 the "James-Lange theory" was published. It set forth James's belief that emotions are organic sensations aroused by bodily expression—that we feel sorry because we cry, and angry because we strike. William James's most important work, *The Principles of Psychology* was published in 1890. In this book, James advocated the new psychology that acknowledged a kinship with science as well as with philosophy. The book immediately became popular with laymen as well as with psychologists.

James's increasing fame made him much in demand as a lecturer. He also wrote *The Varieties of Religious Experience*, published in 1902, and *Pragmatism* (1907). In the latter book, he expounded the theory that man knows the true meaning of an idea only when he sees what its effects are. In 1907 James taught his last course at Harvard. He died in Chocorua, N.H., on Aug. 26, 1910.

IMMANUEL KANT

(b. 1724– d. 1804)

I mmanuel Kant was born on April 22, 1724, in Königsberg, Ger. (now Kaliningrad, Russ.). Kant set forth a chain of explosive ideas that humanity has continued to think about since his time. He created a link between the idealists—those who thought that all reality was in the mind—and the materialists—those who thought that the only reality lay in the things of the material world. Kant's ideas on the relationship of mind and matter provide the key to understanding the writings of many 20th-century philosophers.

Painting by Gottlieb Doebler depicting the philosopher Immanuel Kant. Kirsten Neumann/AFP/Getty Images

Kant's father was a saddle and harness maker. He attended school at the Collegium Fredericianum where he studied religion and the Latin classics. When he was 16 years old Kant entered the University of Königsberg. He enrolled as a student of theology but soon became more interested in physics and mathematics.

After leaving college he worked for nine years as a tutor in the homes of wealthy families. In 1755 he earned his doctorate at the university and became a lecturer to university students, living on the small fees his students paid him. He turned down offers from schools that would have taken him elsewhere, and finally the University of Königsberg offered him the position of professor of logic and metaphysics.

Kant never married and he never traveled farther than 50 miles (80 kilometers) from Königsberg. He divided his time among lectures, writing, and daily walks. He was small, thin, and weak, but his ideas were powerful.

Kant's most famous work was the *Critique of Pure Reason* (published in German in 1781). In it he tried to set up the difference between things of the outside world and actions of the mind. He said that things that exist in the world are real, but the human mind is needed to give them order and form and to see the relationships between them. Only the mind can surround them with space and time. The principles of mathematics are part of the space-time thoughts supplied by the mind to real things.

For example, we see only one or two walls of a house at any one time. The mind gathers up these sense impressions of individual walls and mentally builds a complete house. Thus the whole house is being created in the mind while our eyes see only a part of the whole.

Kant said that thoughts must be based on real things. Pure reason without reference to the outside world is impossible. We know only what we first gather up with our senses. Yet living in the real world does not mean that ideals should be abandoned. In his *Critique of Practical Reason* (1788) he argued for a stern morality. His basic idea was in the form of a categorical imperative. This meant that humans should act so well that their conduct could give rise to a universal law. Kant died in Königsberg on Feb. 12, 1804. His last words were *"Es ist gut,"* ("It is good.")

SØREN KIERKEGAARD

(b. 1813 – d. 1855)

Neglected in his lifetime, or ridiculed as a dangerous fanatic, the Danish religious philosopher Kierkegaard came to be regarded in the 20th century as one of the most influential and profound of modern thinkers. He was the most brilliant interpreter of Protestant Christianity in the 19th century. He is generally considered the founder of existentialism, a philosophy that in its simplest terms seeks to explain the significance of the freedom of an individual human being within his or her time on Earth.

Søren Aabye Kierkegaard was born in Copenhagen on May 5, 1813. His prosperous father died in 1838, leaving his two sons an inheritance that freed them from the need to work. Søren was able to devote most of his life to studying and writing. He studied philosophy and theology at the University of Copenhagen.

Kierkegaard was a prolific writer. His subject matter encompassed three basic areas: consideration of the function of the individual human life; vehement opposition to the philosophy of G.W.F. Hegel, whose thought dominated 19th-century Europe; and a clear delineation of Christianity in opposition to the secularism of the state church of Denmark.

Kierkegaard's major works on the human predicament are *Either/Or*, published in 1843, *Fear and Trembling* (1843), *The Concept of Dread* (1844), and *Stages on Life's Way* (1845). His two primary religious-philosophical works, including the attack on Hegel, are *Philosophical Fragments* (1844) and *Concluding Unscientific Postscript to the Philosophical Fragments* (1846). His works on Christianity include *Edifying Discourses in Divers Spirits* (1847), *Works of Love* (1847), *The Sickness unto Death* (1849), and *Training in Christianity* (1850). His last major work, *Attack upon Christendom* (1855), was a strong, satirical attack on the Lutheran state church of Denmark.

Throughout his career, Kierkegaard led a sort of double life. To his friends he was witty, charming, and brilliant in conversation, but by himself he was thoroughly melancholy. Kierkegaard died on Nov. 11, 1855, in Copenhagen. Although his works were known in Denmark and Germany in the late 19th century, it was not until after World War II that interest in them became widespread in Europe and the United States. Among the 20th-century philosophers and theologians influenced by Kierkegaard's work were Karl Barth, Karl Jaspers, Martin Heidegger, and Martin Buber.

AL-KINDI

(b. ?–d. 870)

Ya'ūb ibn Isḥāq aṣ-Ṣabāḥ al-Kindī was the first outstanding Islamic philosopher, known as "the philosopher of the Arabs."

Al-Kindī was born of noble Arabic descent and flourished in Iraq under the caliphs al-Ma'mūn (813–833) and al-Mu'taṣim (833–842). He concerned himself not only with those philosophical questions that had been treated by the Aristotelian Neoplatonists of Alexandria but also with miscellaneous subjects such as astrology, medicine, Indian arithmetic, logogriphs, the manufacture of swords, and cooking. He is known to have written more than 270 works (mostly short treatises), a considerable number of which are extant, and some in Latin translations.

NISHIDA KITARO

(b. 1870– d. 1945)

Nishida Kitaro was born on April 19, 1870, near Kanazawa, Japan. Kitaro was the leading Japanese Buddhist scholar of the 20th-century. He studied at Tokyo University and served as a professor of philosophy at Kyoto University from 1913 to 1928. His writings attempt to assimilate Western philosophy into Buddhist theology. His books include *Philosophical Essays*, *A Study of Good*, and *From the Acting to the Seeing Self*. He died at Kamakura on June 7, 1945.

SAUL KRIPKE

(b. 1940–d.)

Saul Aaron Kripke was born on Nov. 13, 1940, in Bay Shore, L.I., N.Y. He is an American logician and philosopher who from the 1960s has been one of the most powerful thinkers in Anglo-American philosophy.

Kripke began his important work on the semantics of modal logic (the logic of modal notions such as necessity and possibility) while he was still a high-school student in Omaha, Neb. A groundbreaking paper from this period, "A Completeness Theorem for Modal Logic," was published in the *Journal of Symbolic Logic* in 1959, during Kripke's freshman year at Harvard University. In 1962 he graduated from Harvard with the only non-honorary degree he ever received, a B. S. in mathematics. He remained at Harvard until 1968, first as a member of the Harvard Society of Fellows and then as a lecturer.

Kripke taught logic and philosophy at Rockefeller University from 1968 to 1976 and at Princeton University, as McCosh Professor of Philosophy, from 1976 until his retirement in 1998. He delivered the prestigious John Locke Lectures at the University of Oxford in 1973 and received the Rolf Schock Prize in logic and philosophy, awarded by the Royal Swedish Academy of Sciences, in 2001. In 2003 he was appointed distinguished professor at the City University of New York (CUNY).

Kripke's most important philosophical publication, *Naming and Necessity* (1980), based on transcripts of three lectures he delivered at Princeton in 1970 changed the course of analytic philosophy. It provided the first cogent account of necessity and possibility as metaphysical concepts.

Kripke revived the ancient doctrine of essentialism, according to which objects possess certain properties necessarily—without them the objects would not exist at all. On the basis of this doctrine and revolutionary new ideas about the meaning and reference of proper names and of common nouns denoting "natural kinds" (such as heat, water, and tiger), he argued forcefully that some propositions are necessarily true but knowable only a posteriori—e.g., "Water is H_2O" and "Heat is mean molecular kinetic energy"—and that some propositions are contingently true (true in some circumstances but not others) but knowable a priori.

Naming and Necessity also had far-reaching implications regarding the question of whether linguistic meaning and the contents of beliefs and other mental states are partly constituted by social and environmental facts external to the individual. Kripke's work contributed greatly to the decline of ordinary language philosophy and related schools, which held that philosophy is nothing more than the logical analysis of language.

In 1975–76 Kripke published important work on the notion of truth and the liar paradox. Kripke's approach relied on certain previously known conditions under which languages can contain their own truth predicates and on his own intuitive conception of true as a predicate that is only partially defined. Although certain problems arising from the liar paradox remained recalcitrant, Kripke's framework succeeded in inspiring and guiding much subsequent work.

In his later years Kripke wrote several influential papers on linguistic meaning and language use. "Speaker's Reference and Semantic Reference" (1977), for example, explained discrepancies between what the rules of a language determine the referent of a term to be and what speakers use the term to refer to in particular cases. "A Puzzle About Belief" (1979) generated surprising and paradoxical conclusions from seemingly innocent applications of the principles employed in reporting the beliefs of others, and it derived cautionary lessons about attempts to infer facts about linguistic meaning from analyses of belief-reporting sentences.

In *Wittgenstein: On Rules and Private Language* (1982), Kripke used considerations originating in the *Philosophical Investigations* (1953) of Ludwig Wittgenstein to raise skeptical questions about whether knowledge of linguistic meaning can be reduced to rule following, or indeed to any objective facts about speakers

Although a prolific thinker and problem solver, Kripke chose to publish relatively few of his works. Nevertheless, some of his unpublished papers—on recursion theory, truth, the nature of logic, personal identity, the ontological nature of numbers, color and color terms, presupposition, and various paradoxes—have been influential through lectures, seminars, and informal circulation among colleagues and students.

THOMAS KUHN

(b. 1922 – d. 1996)

Thomas Samuel Kuhn was born on July 18, 1922, in Cincinnati, Ohio. He was an American historian of science noted for *The Structure of Scientific Revolutions* (1962), one of the most influential works of history and philosophy written in the 20th century.

Kuhn earned bachelor's (1943) and master's (1946) degrees in physics at Harvard University but obtained his Ph.D. (1949) there in the history of science. He taught the history or philosophy of science at Harvard (1951–56), the University of California at Berkeley (1956–64), Princeton University (1964–79), and the Massachusetts Institute of Technology (1979–91).

In his first book, *The Copernican Revolution* (1957), Kuhn studied the development of the heliocentric theory of the solar system during the Renaissance. In his landmark second book, *The Structure of Scientific Revolutions*, he argued that scientific research and thought are defined by "paradigms," or conceptual world-views, that consist of formal theories, classic experiments, and trusted methods. Scientists typically accept a prevailing paradigm and try to extend its scope by refining theories, explaining puzzling data, and establishing more precise measures of standards and phenomena. Eventually, however, their efforts may generate insoluble theoretical problems or experimental anomalies that expose a paradigm's inadequacies or contradict it altogether. This accumulation of difficulties triggers a crisis that can only be resolved by an intellectual revolution that replaces an old paradigm with a new one.

The overthrow of Ptolemaic cosmology by Copernican heliocentrism, as well as the displacement of Newtonian mechanics

Mutiple-exposure image of Thomas Kuhn—an optical representation of Kuhn's philosophical concept of paradigm shift. Bill Pierce/Time & Life Pictures/Getty Images

by quantum physics and general relativity, are both examples of major paradigm shifts.

Kuhn questioned the traditional conception of scientific progress as a gradual, cumulative acquisition of knowledge based on rationally chosen experimental frameworks. Instead, he argued that the paradigm determines the kinds of experiments scientists perform, the types of questions they ask, and the problems they consider important. A shift in the paradigm alters the fundamental concepts underlying research and inspires new standards of evidence, new research techniques, and new pathways of theory and experiment that are radically incommensurate with the old ones.

Kuhn's book revolutionized the history and philosophy of science, and his concept of paradigm shifts was extended to such disciplines as political science, economics, sociology, and even to business management. Kuhn's later works were a collection of essays, *The Essential Tension* (1977), and the technical study *Black-Body Theory and the Quantum Discontinuity* (1978).

GOTTFRIED WILHELM LEIBNIZ

(b. 1646–d. 1716)

Gottfried Wilhelm Leibniz was born in Leipzig, Ger., on July 1, 1646. Although he was not an artist, Leibniz was in many other ways comparable to Leonardo da Vinci. He was recognized as the universal genius of his time, a philosopher and scientist who worked in the fields of mathematics, geology, theology, mechanics, history, jurisprudence, and linguistics.

He was educated at the University of Leipzig and received a doctorate in law at the University of Nuremberg. Because he was forced to earn a living, he spent his entire adult life in the service of nobility and royalty, particularly for the House of Brunswick-Lüneberg in Germany. His last employer was Duke George Louis of Hanover, who became King George I of England in 1714. This employment enabled Leibniz to travel a great deal throughout Europe and meet the leading scholars of his day. His many duties did not interfere with his extensive intellectual interests.

Gottfried Wilhelm Leibniz monument in his native Leipzig, Ger. Uwe Bumann/ Shutterstock.com

During his lifetime Leibniz perfected the calculating machine invented by Blaise Pascal. He laid the ground for integral and differential calculus and founded dynamics, an area of mechanics. Leibniz then worked on mechanical devices such as clocks, hydraulic presses, lamps, submarines, and windmills and perfected the binary system of numeration used today in computer operation. He also devised the theory that all reasoning can be reduced to an ordered combination of elements such as numbers, words, sounds, or colors (the theoretical basis of modern computers).

Leibniz laid the foundation for general topology, a branch of mathematics, strove to formulate a basis for the unification of the churches and pursued the goal of writing a universal history. He also continued to perfect his metaphysical system through research into the notion of a universal cause of all being.

Leibniz published his philosophy in several works. *Reflections on Knowledge, Truth, and Ideas* defined his theory of knowledge. In *On the Ultimate Origin of Things* he tried to prove that only God could be the source of all things. *Theodicy*, his only major work published in his lifetime, explained his ideas on divine justice. *Monadology*, written two years before his death, spelled out his theory of monads, which he conceived of as simple, un-extended, spiritual substances that formed the basis for all composite forms of reality. His theory of monads—a term derived from the Greek word meaning "that which is one" or "unity"— is elaborated in *Monadology and in Principles of Nature and Grace Founded in Reason.* The theory attempts to describe a harmonious universe made up of an infinite number of monads, or units, arranged in a hierarchy and originating in the Supreme Monad, which is God.

Monadology had its roots in the philosophy of ancient Greece and was carried on by such eminent thinkers as Immanuel Kant, Edmund Husserl, and Alfred North Whitehead. The hierarchy of monadology was, according to Leibniz, the "best of all possible worlds." The philosopher died in Hanover on Nov. 14, 1716.

DAVID KELLOGG LEWIS
(b. 1941 – d. 2001)

D avid Kellogg Lewis was born on Sept. 28, 1941, in Oberlin, Ohio, U.S.A, He was an American philosopher who, at the time of his death, was considered by many to be the leading figure in Anglo-American philosophy.

Both Lewis's father and his mother taught government at Oberlin College. Lewis studied philosophy at Swarthmore College (B.A., 1962) and Harvard University, where he received an M.A. in 1964 and a Ph.D. in 1967. His dissertation on linguistic convention, written under the supervision of Willard Van Orman Quine (1908–2000), was published as *Convention: A Philosophical Study* in 1969. Lewis taught at the University of California, Los Angeles, from 1966 to 1970 and thereafter at Princeton University. He died suddenly and unexpectedly at age 60, at the height of his intellectual powers.

Lewis identified several "recurring themes" that unify his work. Four of these themes are particularly important:

1. There are possible but non-actual things. Non-actual things do not differ from actual things in any fundamentally important way.

2. Temporal relations are strongly analogous to spatial relations. Just as the far side of the Moon is elsewhere in space (relative to an observer on Earth), so things in the past or the future are "elsewhere in time" but are no less real for being so.

3. Physical science, if successful, will provide a complete description of the actual world.

4. Given any possible world in which every inhabitant of that world is in space and time (as is the case in the actual world), everything true about that world and its inhabitants supervenes on—is determined or settled by—the distribution of "local qualities" in space and time in that world.

Two important examples of local-quality supervenience are the mental states of human beings (and other sentient creatures) and causal relations between physical objects or events. Enlightenment philosopher David Hume (1711–76) held that causal relations consist of nothing more than the "constant conjunction" in experience of certain kinds of objects or events—Lewis referred to theme 4 as the doctrine of Humean supervenience.

According to Lewis, Humean supervenience faces only one serious challenge: objective chance, or propensity, a notion that Lewis thought was indispensable to science. Objective chance is an interpretation of probability as an objective tendency of a physical situation to produce an outcome of a certain kind. The problem is that there appear to be instances of objective chance that are not interpretable in this way. After many years of thought, Lewis finally arrived at what he considered a satisfactory solution the details of which were presented in a paper titled "Humean Supervenience Debugged" (1994).

Lewis regarded his doctrine of non-actual things and worlds as a "philosopher's paradise," and much of his work on particular philosophical problems (in metaphysics, the philosophy of language, the philosophy of mind, and epistemology) presupposed the reality of non-actual things. Few philosophers have accepted this presupposition, however; most have regarded it as simply unbelievable. Nevertheless, almost all philosophers who have studied Lewis's work have concluded that there is very little of it that cannot be detached from his doctrine of the non-actual and restated in terms of what they would consider a more plausible theory.

Lewis applied himself to a wide variety of philosophical problems and made important—sometimes groundbreaking—contributions to a number of fields. The topics on which he wrote include analyticity, causation, personal identity over time, freedom of the will, the possibility of time travel, perception and hallucination, truth in fiction, existence and nonexistence, the nature of mathematical objects, universals, and the analysis of knowledge. Only by studying Lewis's work in detail can one appreciate the depth and originality of his thought.

Lewis died on Oct. 14, 2001 in Princeton, N.J.

JOHN LOCKE

(b. 1632 – d. 1704)

John Locke was born in Wrington, Somerset, on August 29, 1632. He was one of the pioneers in modern thinking and made great contributions in studies of politics, government, and psychology.

Locke was the son of a well-to-do Puritan lawyer who fought for Cromwell in the English Civil War. The father, also named John Locke, was a pious, even-tempered man.

The boy was educated at Westminster School and Oxford and later became a tutor at the university. His friends urged him to enter the Church of England, but he decided that he was not fitted for the calling. He had long been interested in meteorology and the experimental sciences, especially chemistry. He turned to medicine and became known as one of the most skilled practitioners of his day.

In 1667 Locke became the personal secretary and physician to Anthony Ashley Cooper, later Lord Chancellor, and the First Earl of Shaftesbury. Locke's association with Shaftesbury enabled him to meet many of the great men of England, but it also caused him a great deal of trouble. Shaftesbury was indicted for high treason. He was acquitted, but Locke was suspected of disloyalty. In 1683 he left England for Holland and returned only after the revolution of 1688.

Locke is remembered today largely as a political philosopher. He preached the doctrine that men naturally possess certain large rights, the chief being life, liberty, and property. Rulers, he said, derived their power only from the consent of the people. He thought that the government should be like a contract between the rulers and his subjects: The people give up certain rights in return for just rule, and the ruler should hold his power only so long as he uses it justly. These ideas had a tremendous effect on all future political thinking. The American Declaration of Independence clearly reflects Locke's teachings.

Locke was always very interested in psychology. About 1670, friends urged him to write a paper on the limitations of human judgment. He started to write a few paragraphs, but 20 years passed before he finished. The result was his great and famous "An Essay Concerning Human Understanding." In this work he stressed the theory that the human mind starts as a tabula rasa(smoothed tablet)—that is, a waxed tablet ready to be used for writing. The mind has no inborn ideas, as most men of the time believed. Throughout life it forms its ideas only from impressions (sense experiences) that are made upon its surface.

In discussing education Locke urged the view that character formation is far more important than information and that learning should be pleasant. During his later years he turned more and more to writing about religion.

The principal works by Locke are letters—"On Toleration" (1689, 1690, 1692); "An Essay Concerning Human Understanding" (1690); two treatises—"On Civil Government" (1690), and "Some Thoughts Concerning Education" (1693); and "The Reasonableness of Christianity" (1695). He died in Oates, Essex, on Oct. 28, 1704.

NICCOLÒ MACHIAVELLI

(b. 1469 – d. 1527)

Niccolò Machiavelli was born in Florence on May 3, 1469. The term "Machiavellian" refers to someone who is cunning, cynical, and unprincipled. The adjective would have dismayed Machiavelli, from whose name it is derived. He was one of the brightest lights of the Italian Renaissance, a writer of powerful, influential, and thoughtful prose who was devoted to truth and to the freedom of Florence, the city he loved.

Machiavelli has been so misunderstood because his chief works—*The Prince* and *Discourses on Livy*, both published in 1513—have been seriously misinterpreted. Machiavelli had a tragic sense of human wickedness. This pessimism often led him to express himself more bluntly than he might otherwise have done. He was, above all, a realist when it came to understanding human nature. His reflections on mankind and its past made him a founder of the philosophy of history.

Because of his family's poverty he received most of his education at home. In 1498 he was given a government position in the city and remained in its service for 13 years.

Machiavelli was frequently used as a roving ambassador, trying to protect the interests of Florence from being sacrificed to the warring parties of Europe: France, the Holy Roman Empire, and the Roman Catholic Church. One of his most vital contributions to the welfare of Florence was persuading the city to raise its own militia instead of using a mercenary, or hired army. He was proved right when his militia helped conquer Pisa in 1509.

When Giuliano de' Medici became ruler of Florence in 1512, Machiavelli lost his post. He went to live on his property outside the city and spent the time writing his two masterpieces as well as a comedy, *The Mandrake* (1518). Cardinal Giulio de' Medici, later Pope Clement VII, came to govern Florence in 1520, and the writer was restored to government service. In honor of his patron, Lorenzo Strozzi, he wrote *On the Art of War* (1521), a treatise that laid the foundations of modern military tactics. When the Medici were cast off in 1527, Machiavelli was again turned out of office because he had served a Medici. He died on June 21, 1527.

Statue of Niccolo Machiavelli, in Florence's Uffizi Gallery museum.
Hulton Archive/Getty Images

MOSES MAIMONIDES

(b. 1135– d. 1204)

Moses Maimonides, also known as Rambam, was born Moses ben Maimon in Córdoba, Spain, on March 30, 1135, to an educated, distinguished family. The main intellectual figure of medieval Judaism, Maimonides was a prolific writer whose ideas about philosophy, religion, and medicine had vast influence. He is best known for three works: his commentary on the Mishna, his code of Jewish law, and his *Guide for the Perplexed*.

In 1159 the family left Spain for Fez, Mor., because of the persecution of the Jews of Córdoba at the hands of a fanatical Islamic sect. In Fez, Maimonides began his study of medicine, but again his family fled persecution and moved to Palestine. They finally settled in the 1160s in Fostat, Egypt, near Cairo. Here they were free to practice Judaism, but soon after their arrival Maimonides's father and brother died, and Maimonides began to practice medicine to support his family. His fame as a physician spread, and he soon became the court physician for Sultan Saladin and his family. Maimonides also lectured at the local hospital, maintained a private practice, and was a leader in the Jewish community.

Maimonides's writings are varied and vast. He believed that reason should guide all things but only as long as the Bible's absolute doctrines are not sacrificed. When he was 23 he began to write a commentary on the Mishna, an authoritative collection of oral laws containing all of the decisions in Jewish law that were compiled from the earliest times to the beginning of the 3rd century CE. Maimonides clarified certain terms and phrases and wrote several introductory essays. One of these essays, Maimonides's "Thirteen Articles of Faith," summarizes the teachings of Judaism.

When he finished this project, he began one of his masterworks, Mishne Torah. This is a code of Jewish law, or Halakah, written in Hebrew. His *Guide for the Perplexed*, written originally in Arabic, took Maimonides 15 years. In it he urges the search for a rational philosophy of Judaism. It is this work that stimulated philosophers and religious scholars for generations afterward. Many of his minor works—including several concerning medicine, astronomy, and physics—are still read and studied. Maimonides died on Dec. 13, 1204, and was buried in Tiberias near the Sea of Galilee.

MARCUS AURELIUS

(b. CE 121–d. CE 180)

A great task faced Marcus Aurelius when he became the Roman emperor in CE 161, as successor to his uncle, Emperor Antonius Pius. Generations of luxury had made the patricians, or nobles, weak and selfish. The middle class was disappearing, and the working class was being reduced to a state of slavery. Germanic tribes were at the borders of the empire, while few Romans seemed willing to defend their homeland.

Marcus Aurelius had been trained in the Greek Stoic philosophy, and he followed it throughout his life. He placed the good of society before his own comfort. He put good government into effect, limited the gladiatorial games, and passed laws that benefited slaves. Although he had noble principles, Marcus Aurelius persecuted the Christians for fear they would destroy the state. Although he loved peace, he was a good warrior and succeeded in defending the border provinces against invasion. In his spare moments he jotted down in Greek the rules that guided his own conduct. The resulting volume of Meditations was for many generations one of the world's most admired books of practical and political wisdom.

Marcus was the last of the "five good emperors," whose combined reigns marked the golden age of the Roman Empire. He died on March 17, 180.

KARL MARX

(b. 1818–d. 1883)

K arl Marx was born on May 5, 1818, in Trier in the German Rhineland. Known during his lifetime only to a small group of socialists and revolutionaries, Marx wrote books now considered by Communists all over the world to be the source of absolute truth on matters of economics, philosophy, and politics. Most modern socialists also base their codes to a lesser or greater degree on Marx's theories.

Marx's grandfather was a rabbi. His father, a successful lawyer, had his entire family baptized for business and social reasons. Marx studied law at Bonn and philosophy at the University of Berlin. While in Berlin he became acquainted with the philosophy of Georg Wilhelm Friedrich Hegel.

At 24 he became editor of a paper in Cologne, Ger. His radical ideas soon got him into censorship trouble, and he went to Paris, partly to escape arrest. With him went his beautiful young wife, Jenny von Westphalen, whom he had married in spite of both families' misgivings.

Expelled from Paris in 1845, Marx lived for a time in Brussels, Bel. He later returned to Paris but was expelled again in 1849. Marx then went to England. He made his home in London for the remaining 34 years of his life. He lived in wretched poverty and spent day after day studying in the British Museum library. He was devoted to his wife and children, but because of his uncompromising nature he had few friends.

One friend, however, remained faithful to him and paid his bills. He was Friedrich Engels, a textile manufacturer whose ideas were in complete accord with Marx's and who collaborated with him in his writing.

While in Brussels Marx and Engels had written the pamphlet "Manifesto of the Communist Party," published in 1848. It contains the simplest expression of Marx's beliefs. The ideas in it were later developed at length in the three volumes of Marx's major work, *Das Kapital* (*Capital*). This also was written in collaboration with Engels, who published the last two volumes after Marx's death. The first volume appeared in 1867.

Marx based his theories on what he believed to be the scientific evidence of history. He searched the past for proof of the continual class struggle between the middle-class exploiters (the bourgeoisie) and the oppressed working people (the proletariat). The final struggle, he predicted, would lead to the overthrow of capitalism and its supporters.

He claimed a classless society would then emerge and there would thus be no more revolutions. Everyone would be guided by the maxim "From each according to his ability, to each according to his needs." The government would no longer be needed and would "wither away." Marx did not concern himself much with practical problems but concentrated only on the revolution itself.

Marx died in London on March 14, 1883. He had outlived his wife and all but two of his six children. Only eight people were present to hear Engels's funeral oration in Highgate Cemetery.

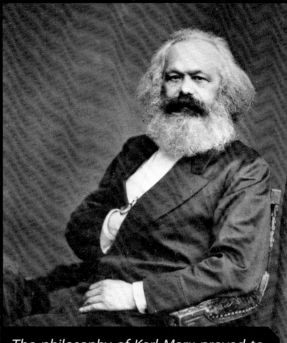

The philosophy of Karl Marx proved to be a driving force behind the Communist Party, as well as modern socialists today. Roger Viollet/Getty Images

MENCIUS

(b. 371? BCE – d. 289? BCE)

Mencius was born as Meng Ke in about 371 BCE in Zou, a minor state in what is now Shandong Province, China. Mencius is considered the "second sage" in Confucianism, after Confucius. Mencius reformulated Confucianism some 150 years after Confucius's death. He is known in Chinese as Mengzi (meaning "Master Meng." His disciples compiled records of his sayings and acts in a book named *Mencius*. A Confucian classic, it forms part of the *Sishu* (Four Books), which are usually the first Confucian texts that Chinese students learn.

Like Confucius, Mencius was only 3 when he lost his father. Mencius's mother is said to have paid special attention to the upbringing of her young son. Among the Chinese, Mencius's mother has been for ages upheld as the model mother.

As a young scholar, Mencius is said to have been taught by a pupil of Confucius' grandson. Mencius ultimately became a teacher himself and for a brief period served as an official in the state of Qi. He spent much of his time traveling from state to state, offering his advice to the various princes on government by *ren* (human-heartedness), or humane government. The effort was doomed to fail because the times were chaotic: Mencius lived during part of the Zhou Dynasty known as the Warring States period (475–221 BCE), during which the princes of several rival states fought each other for supremacy.

Mencius patiently urged the princes to live virtuously and to forsake the use of force. At the time, rulers in China were believed to govern by a "mandate of heaven." Mencius emphatically reminded the princes of the responsibility that came with this mandate for them to govern for the good of the people. According to Mencius, a ruler was to provide for the welfare of the people both in material conditions for their livelihood and in moral and educational guidance.

A ruler, who did not so govern, should be criticized, rehabilitated, or, as a last resort, deposed. Mencius also advocated light taxes, free trade, conservation of natural resources, welfare measures for the old and disadvantaged, and equal sharing of wealth. The outspoken sympathies of Mencius made him a champion of the common people and an advocate of democratic principles in government.

Mencius was unable to find a prince willing to put his principles of government into practice. His sense of disappointment grew, and he finally returned to his native state of Zou. There he devoted the remaining years of his life to teaching.

The philosophy of Mencius can be regarded as an amplification of the teachings of Confucius. Confucius taught the concept of ren, love or human-heartedness, as the basic virtue.

While Mencius has always been regarded as a major philosopher, special importance was attributed to him by the Neo-Confucianists of the Song Dynasty, which lasted from 960 to 1279. For the last 1,000 years, Mencius has been revered as the cofounder of Confucianism, second only to Confucius himself.

MOSES MENDELSSOHN

(b. 1729 – d. 1786)

Moses Mendelssohn was born on Sept. 26, 1729, in Dessau, Anhalt (now eastern Germany), the son of a poor scribe. The greatest of 18th-century Jewish philosophers, Moses Mendelssohn influenced Immanuel Kant and a generation of German philosophers as well as the course of Jewish philosophy. His collected works fill seven volumes and were published in 1843–45.

He studied German and Latin and was introduced to the philosophy of Maimonides by his teacher David Fränkel. He followed Fränkel to Berlin, where he became acquainted with Gotthold Ephraim Lessing, who modeled the central figure of his drama Nathan the Wise after Mendelssohn.

In 1763 Mendelssohn won a prize in a literary contest of the Prussian Academy of Arts. As a result King Frederick the Great of Prussia deemed him a "privileged Jew" who would not suffer the usual burdens placed on Jews.

In 1767 Mendelssohn wrote his celebrated work *Phaedo, or On the Immortality of the Soul*. In 1780 he began work on his translation of the Pentateuch (the first five books of the Bible). The translation was written in German and printed with Hebrew characters, and it was considered a stepping-stone to the German language and life beyond the ghetto. *Morning Hours*, written in 1785, supports the beliefs of German philosopher Gottfried Wilhelm Leibniz and was written in defense of Lessing. Mendelssohn struggled to find a way for Jews to adhere to German society while maintaining their Jewish values. He died in Berlin on Jan. 4, 1786. His grandson was Felix Mendelssohn, the composer.

JOHN STUART MILL

(b. 1806 – d. 1873)

John Stuart Mill was born in London on May 20, 1806. Mill was an English author, philosopher, economist, and reformer. Mill wrote

79

on subjects that ranged from women's suffrage to political ethics. His works, while influential, have been described as revealing only some aspects of the author's mind. More notable, critics have said, was his absolute fairness. He not only welcomed ideas that opposed his own but also, if convinced, adopted them. A political theorist, he enjoyed the challenge of day-to-day business and government.

He received an exclusive education from his father, James Mill, who taught the boy Latin, Greek, geometry, algebra, and history. By his eighth year John had read Aesop's fables and other works in the original Greek. After a year in France (1820–21), during which he studied chemistry, botany, and mathematics, Mill took a post with the India House, head-quarters of the British East India Company, where his father worked. He suffered a mental breakdown three years later but recovered to begin studying the arts.

Photograph of English philosopher and reformer John Stuart Mill. London Stereoscopic Company/Hulton Archive/ Getty Images

Mill became assistant examiner of the India House in 1828 and had charge of the British East India Company's relations with the Indian states from 1836, when his father died, to 1856. A long friendship with Mrs. Harriet Hardy Taylor led, after her husband's death, to their marriage in 1851. Influenced by Jeremy Bentham, Mill became a utilitarian accept-ing the principle of "the greatest good for the great-est number" of people. He published his *System of Logic* (1843); *Principles of Political Economy* (1848); *On Liberty* (1859), a book that he revised with his wife's help; *The Subjection of Women* (1869);

and many other works. In 1858 he made his home in Avignon, France, where his wife died a short time later. Back in England in 1865, he was elected to Parliament and served until 1868. He returned to Avignon, where he died on May 8, 1873.

MONTESQUIEU

(b. 1689 – d. 1755)

Charles-Louis de Secondat or the baron of Montesquieu was born on Jan. 18, 1689, near Bordeaux, France. A French political philosopher, Montesquieu developed the theory that governmental powers should be divided between executive, legislative, and judicial bodies. In the late 1780s his theory became a reality when it was adopted as one of the fundamental principles of the U.S. governmental system.

He was educated at the College de Juilly and studied law at the University of Bordeaux. When his uncle died in 1716, Charles-Louis became the baron of Montesquieu.

In 1721 Montesquieu published his first book, *Lettres Persanes* (*Persian Letters*), which used the experiences of two fictitious Persian travelers to poke fun at the French government and social classes. The following year he went to Paris, where he moved in court circles, and in 1728 he became a member of the Académie Française, a prestigious intellectual society. Montesquieu sought to increase his knowledge by traveling through Europe.

Upon his return he began a major work on law and politics, comparing the governments of various countries. In 1748, after years of work, *L'Esprit des lois* (*The Spirit of Laws*) appeared. To Montesquieu, abuse of power, slavery, and intolerance were evil. His book reflects his idea that government can avoid these evils by separating power into executive, legislative, and judicial branches, by governing with honor rather than through fear, and by upholding human dignity.

His book was controversial but also very influential. It inspired France's Declaration of the Rights of Man and the U.S. Constitution. Montesquieu published a defense of *L'Esprit des lois* in 1750 and in his last years was a contributor to the *Encyclopédie*. He died in Paris on Feb. 10, 1755.

G. E. MOORE

(b. 1873 – d. 1958)

G. E. Moore was born on November 4, 1873 in London, Eng. He was an influential British Realist philosopher and professor whose systematic approach to ethical problems and remarkably meticulous approach to philosophy made him an outstanding modern British thinker.

Elected to a fellowship at Trinity College, Cambridge, in 1898, Moore remained there until 1904, during which time he published several journal articles, including "The Nature of Judgment" (1899) and "The Refutation of Idealism" (1903), as well as his major ethical work, *Principia Ethica* (1903). These writings were important in helping to undermine the influence of Hegel and Kant on British philosophy. After residence in Edinburgh and London, he returned to Cambridge in 1911 to become a lecturer in moral science. From 1925 to 1939 he was professor of philosophy there, and from 1921 to 1947 he was editor of the philosophical journal *Mind*.

Though Moore grew up in a climate of evangelical religiosity, he eventually became an agnostic. A friend of Bertrand Russell, who first directed him to the study of philosophy, he was also a leading figure in the Bloomsbury group, a close-knit group that included the economist John Keynes and the writers Virginia Woolf and E.M. Forster. Because of his view that "the good" is knowable by direct apprehension, he became known as an "ethical intuitionist." He claimed that other efforts to decide what is "good," such as analyses of the concepts of approval or desire, which are not themselves of an ethical nature, partake of a fallacy that he termed the "naturalistic fallacy."

Moore was also preoccupied with such problems as the nature of sense perception and the existence of other minds and material things. He was not as skeptical as those philosophers who held that we lack sufficient data to prove that objects exist outside our own minds, but he did believe that proper philosophical proofs had not yet been devised to overcome such objections.

Although few of Moore's theories achieved general acceptance, his unique approaches to certain problems and his intellectual rigor helped change the texture of philosophical discussion in England. His other major writings include *Philosophical Studies* (1922) and *Some Main Problems of Philosophy* (1953); posthumous publications were *Philosophical Papers* (1959) and the *Commonplace Book, 1919–1953* (1962).

Moore died on died Oct. 24, 1958, in Cambridge, Cambridgeshire.

NAGARJUNA

(fl. 2nd century CE)

Nagarjuna was an Indian Buddhist philosopher who articulated the doctrine of emptiness (*shunyata*) and is traditionally regarded as the founder of the Madhyamika ("Middle Way") school, of Mahayana Buddhist philosophy.

Very little can be said concerning his life; scholars generally place him in South India during the 2nd century CE. Traditional accounts state that he lived 400 years after the Buddha passed into Nirvana (*c*.5th–4th century BCE). Some biographies also state, however, that he lived for 600 years, apparently identifying him with a second Nagarjuna known for his Tantric writings.

Although he is best known in the West for his writings on emptiness, especially as set forth in his most famous work, the *Madhyamika-shastra* ("Treatise on the Middle Way," also known as the *Mulamadhyamakakarika*, "Fundamental Verses on the Middle Way"), Nagarjuna wrote many other works on a wide range of topics (even when questions of attribution are taken into account).

Nagarjuna wrote as a Buddhist monk and as a proponent of the Mahayana (Sanskrit: "Greater Vehicle") school, which emphasized the idea of the "bodhisattva," or one who seeks to become a Buddha.

He compiled an anthology, entitled the *Sutrasamuccaya* ("Compendium of Sutras"), consisting of passages from 68 sutras, most of which were Mahayana texts. Nagarjuna is particularly associated with the Prajnaparamita ("Perfection of Wisdom") sutras in this corpus. According to legend, he retrieved from the bottom of the sea a perfection-of-wisdom sutra that the Buddha had entrusted to the king of the nagas (water deities) for safekeeping. Nagarjuna also composed hymns of praise to the Buddha and expositions of Buddhist ethical practice.

Despite his monastic background, Nagarjuna addressed his works to a variety of audiences. His philosophical texts were sometimes directed against logicians of non-Buddhist schools, but most often they offered critiques of the doctrines and assumptions of the non-Mahayana Buddhist schools, especially the Sarvastivada (literally, "Asserting Everything That Exists").

In his first sermon, the Buddha prescribed a "middle way" between the extremes of self-indulgence and self-mortification. Nagarjuna, citing an early sutra, expanded the notion of the middle way into the philosophical sphere, identifying a middle way between existence and non-existence, or between permanence and annihilation.

Nagarjuna developed his doctrine of emptiness in the *Madhyamika-shastra*, a thoroughgoing analysis of a wide range of topics. Examining, among other things, the Buddha, the Four Noble Truths, and nirvana, Nagarjuna demonstrates that each lacks the autonomy and independence that is falsely ascribed to it. For Nagarjuna, the impossibility of such production is confirmed in the Prajnaparamita sutras by the claim that all phenomena are *anutpada* ("unproduced").

Nagarjuna defined emptiness in terms of the doctrine of *pratitya-samutpada* ("dependent origination"), He employs the doctrine of the two truths, *paramartha satya* ("ultimate truth") and *samvriti satya* ("conventional truth"), explaining that everything that exists is ultimately empty of any intrinsic nature but does exist conventionally.

Nagarjuna is the most famous thinker in the history of Buddhism after the Buddha himself. As more works of Nagarjuna were studied, he came to be understood more clearly within the philosophical and religious milieu in which he lived.

FRIEDRICH NIETZSCHE

(b. 1844 – d. 1900)

Friedrich Nietzsche was a man of the 19th century whose influence on 20th-century thought was enormous. It was not so much what Friedrich Nietzsche believed as what he saw happening in European civilization that was so meaningful in later decades.

Nietzche was born in Röcken in the Prussian province of Saxony on Oct. 15, 1844. He attended the universities of Bonn and Leipzig to study classical literature and language, and his brilliance brought him a professorship at the University of Basel in Switzerland. He was there from 1869 to 1879 except for brief military service in the Franco-Prussian War. His first great work—*The Birth of Tragedy* (1872)—was followed by *Thoughts out of Season* (1873–76), a collection of essays, and *Human, All Too Human* (1878), a book of sayings.

Pleading ill health, he left Basel and began the period of his greatest creativity, which lasted until mental illness overcame him in 1889. His later works included *Thus Spake Zarathustra* (published over a period of years), *Beyond Good and Evil* (1886), *On the Genealogy of Morals* (1887), *Twilight of the Idols* (1889), and *The Antichrist* (1895).

Nietzsche saw a civilization so self-confident over its mastery of science, technology,

Photograph of German philosopher Friedrich Nietzsche. Library of Congress Prints and Photographs Division

politics, and economics that for it "God is dead," and that "belief in the Christian God has become unworthy of belief." Nietzsche saw emerging tensions arising from those who embraced democracy, socialism, or Communism. He predicted: "There will be wars such as there have never been on Earth before." His death in Weimar, Ger., on Aug. 25, 1900, prevented him from witnessing the accuracy of his predictions.

For years after his death Nietzsche's name was mistakenly associated with Adolf Hitler and fascism. Nietzsche's sister, Elisabeth, changed his writings to reflect her own anti-Semitic, nationalistic ideas. Critics were misled by her forgeries and linked Nietzsche with the Nazis.

ROBERT NOZICK

(b. 1938 – d. 2002)

U.S. philosopher, Robert Nozick was born in Brooklyn, N.Y., and graduated from Columbia University in 1959, having become a Socialist and student radical in the process. He earned a doctorate from Princeton in 1963, and studied at Oxford in England from 1963 to 64. He then taught at Princeton and Rockefeller universities before joining faculty of Harvard in 1965. Nozick is best known for his controversial book *Anarchy, State, and Utopia* (1975), which promoted radical libertarian political views. He published *Philosophical Explanations* in 1981, *The Examined Life* in 1989, *The Nature of Rationality* in 1993, *Socratic Puzzles* in 1996, and *Invariances: The Structure of the Objective World* in 2001. Nozick died in Cambridge, Mass., on January 23, 2002.

WILLIAM OF OCKHAM

(b. 1285 – d. 1347/49?)

William of Ockham was born in about 1285, probably in Surrey, Eng. His reputation in philosophy and theology had never been as great as that of his 13th-century predecessor Thomas Aquinas. The reason is that Ockham stood outside the mainstream of Catholic thought in his lifetime. As a youth he entered the Franciscan order and remained in it his whole life. His first love was logic, which he studied thoroughly. A philosophical principle called "Ockham's razor" has been attributed to him. It says: Do not give more explanations than necessary for any given situation.

Ockham studied theology at Oxford University, but he was forced to leave the school when his fellow theologians denounced his ideas. He fled to Avignon, France, where he became involved in the conflict over poverty between the pope and the Franciscans. He fled Avignon because of papal hostility and settled in Munich, Bavaria. There he continued to write on logic and against the church's vast wealth until his death, probably from bubonic plague, in either 1347 or 1349.

PARMENIDES

(b. 515 BCE – d. ?)

P armenides was a Greek philosopher of Elea in southern Italy who founded Eleaticism, one of the leading pre-Socratic schools of Greek thought. His general teaching has been diligently reconstructed from the few surviving fragments of his principal work, a lengthy three-part verse composition titled *On Nature*.

Parmenides held that the multiplicity of existing things, their changing forms and motion, are but an appearance of a single eternal reality ("Being"), thus giving rise to the Parmenidean principle that "all is one." From this concept of Being, he went on to say that all claims of change or of non-Being are illogical. Because he introduced the method of basing claims about appearances on a logical concept of Being, he is considered one of the founders of metaphysics. Plato's dialogue the *Parmenides* deals with his thought.

PHILO JUDAEUS

(b. 15 BCE – d. CE 50)

D uring the first decades of the 1st century CE, the writings of Philo created a bridge between Judaism and Greek philosophy. Part of his work represents the largest commentary on Jewish law prior to the creation of the Talmud. He was well schooled in the philosophies of Plato, Aristotle, the Cynics, the Stoics, and other Greek thought. His blending of Plato with Biblical concepts was especially valuable to early Christian writers.

Philo was a Jew who lived in Alexandria, Egypt, one of the vital centers of learning and culture in the Roman Empire. Of Philo's life, very little is known. He was born in Alexandria sometime between 15 and 10 BCE and died there sometime between CE 45 and 50. He probably studied arithmetic, philosophy, geometry, astronomy, harmonics, grammar, rhetoric, and logic. Of any special Jewish education he says very little in his writings. He was nevertheless quite familiar with the religious traditions of ancient Israel and had a complete knowledge of the Hebrew Bible (called the Old Testament by Christians). The only well-known event of his life was an appearance about CE 39 before the emperor Caligula in Rome to defend the Jews of Alexandria after a period of persecution.

Philo's writings fall into three categories: religious essays based on the first five books of the Bible, general religious and philosophical essays, and writings of topical events. These works include *Allegories of the Laws*, *On the Eternity of the Word*, and *Suppositions*, a defense against anti-Semitism. Plato had stated that only eternal ideas are real. The material world, because it is changing and temporary, is a product of eternal ideas. Philo said that the ideas existed first in the mind of God. Because Philo believed that God is completely remote and unknowable, he suggested that there is a second God, an intermediary between God and creation. He named this intermediary Logos, a Greek word he interpreted as the totality of the eternal ideas and the creative power that made the universe. Christians later identified the Logos with Jesus, not as a second God but as God's self-revelation. Philo believed that humans have free will. His belief that the body was the prison house of the soul influenced later Gnosticism. He embraced democracy as the best form of government, saying all people should be equal before the law. Unlike Plato, he said happiness is a gift of God, not the result of pursuing virtue.

PLATO

(b. 428? BCE – d. 348? BCE)

Plato was born in Athens in about 428 BCE and grew up during the decades of conflict with Sparta and other city-states. "The safest general characterization of the European philosophical tradition is that it consists of a series of footnotes to Plato." This assessment by the 20th-century philosopher-mathematician Alfred North Whitehead can be considered only a slight exaggeration. The religious traditions of Judaism and Christianity have provided one foundation of Western civilization, while the Greek philosophers Socrates, Plato, and Aristotle have provided another.

The influence of Plato has been persistent and unbroken. His Academy at Athens, which opened in about 387 BCE, was the first forerunner of today's colleges and universities. It was a school devoted to philosophy, law, and scientific research—primarily mathematics—and it endured as an institution until CE 529, when it and other non-Christian schools were closed by the emperor Justinian.

Plato's influence extended far beyond the Academy. In his lifetime he was the most celebrated teacher of his day. After his death his ideas were taken up by countless other thinkers. Philo of Alexandria used Plato's ideas to give a philosophical framework to Judaism. Early Christian writers eagerly embraced Plato's thought as the best available instrument for explaining and defending the teachings of the Bible and church tradition. Of the Christian Platonists, St. Augustine of Hippo was the best known and most influential. Plato's influence spread into Islam as well, through the writings of the philosophers Avicenna and Averroës.

His parents, Ariston and Perictione, were one of the most distinguished and aristocratic couples in the city. Of the details of Plato's early life almost nothing is known. Because of his family's position it is likely that he was acquainted with Socrates from childhood. Plato probably intended to go into politics, but the fate that Socrates met at the hands of Athenian politicians changed his mind.

Statue of the ancient Greek phi-losopher Plato, in the main reading room of the United States Library of Congress. Library of Congress Prints and Photographs Division

With the forced suicide of Socrates in 399, Plato and other followers took temporary refuge in Megara. Some early biographers say that he then traveled around the Mediterranean world, visiting other Greek city-states, Egypt, Italy, and Sicily. None of the reports can be confirmed except for a trip to Sicily. There he met and befriended Dion, brother-in-law of the ruler of Syracuse, Dionysius I. Sometime after the death of Socrates, Plato decided to devote himself to philosophy and teaching. He opened the Academy and remained with it as teacher, with two brief interruptions, until his death in about 348 BCE.

The interruptions had to do with the government in Syracuse. Dionysius I died in 367 and was succeeded by Dionysius II, an uneducated youth. Dion called on Plato to come to Syracuse to teach the new ruler. Plato agreed, but the cause proved hopeless and he returned to Athens. He made one more journey to Syracuse in 361–360.

Plato's complete body of work has come down to the present. No genuine writing was lost, though a number of false writings were passed along as his. If the *Epistles* are considered one item, there are 36 works. All, except for the letters, are called dialogues because they are presented mostly in conversational style as discussions between two or more individuals. One of the masterpieces of world literature is the *Republic*. Like the *Laws*—Plato's last work—it is book length, while many others are much shorter.

The earliest dialogues were those in which Socrates takes the lead in conversation. The shorter ones usually deal with one issue. The *Lysis*, for instance, examines the nature of friendship, while the *Meno* is a discussion of virtue. The *Apology* is the last statement of Socrates about his life and work through speeches at his trial for impiety.

The *Republic* discusses the nature of justice and the institutions of society. In some ways it is utopian in that it describes Plato's ideal society. But it also deals with the whole range of human knowledge, the purpose and content of education, and the nature of science. Much of it is a treatise in which three types of lives are distinguished. The philosopher is devoted to attaining wisdom, the hedonist seeks only pleasure and self-gratification, and the man of action desires recognition for his practical abilities.

PLOTINUS

(b. 205 CE – d. 270 CE)

P lotinus was born in 205 CE, Lyco, or Lycopolis in Egypt. He was an ancient philosopher, the center of an influential circle of intellectuals and men of letters in 3rd-century Rome, who is regarded by modern scholars as the founder of the Neo-platonic school of philosophy.

The only important source for the life of Plotinus is the biography that his disciple and editor Porphyry wrote as a preface to his edition of the writings of his master, the *Enneads*. Porphyry concentrates on the last six years, when he was with his master in Rome. Thus, a fairly complete picture is available only of the last six years of a man who died at the age of 65. According to Porphyry, Plotinus never spoke about his parents, his race, or his country.

In his 28th year—he seems to have been rather a late developer—Plotinus felt an impulse to study philosophy and thus went to Alexandria. When Plotinuss heard Ammonius speak, he said, "This is the man I was looking for," and stayed with him for 11 years.

At the end of his time with Ammonius, Plotinus joined the expedition of the Roman emperor Gordian III against Persia (242–243), with the intention of trying to learn something firsthand about the philosophies of the Persians and Indians. The expedition came to a disastrous end in Mesopotamia, however, when Gordian was murdered by the soldiers and Philip the Arabian was proclaimed emperor. Plotinus escaped with difficulty and made his way back to Antioch. From there he went to Rome, where he settled at the age of 40.

By the time Porphyry made his acquaintance in 263 he was living in dignified and comfortable conditions. His reputation in society was excellent. He acted as an arbitrator in disputes without ever being known to make an enemy, and many of his aristocratic friends, when they were approaching death, appointed him guardian of their children.

Plotinus' main activity, to which he devoted most of his time and energy, was his teaching and after his first 10 years in Rome, his writing. There was nothing academic or highly organized about his "school," though his method of teaching was rather scholastic. He would have passages read from commentaries on Plato or Aristotle by earlier philosophers and then expound his own views. The meetings, however, were friendly and informal, and Plotinus encouraged unlimited discussion. Difficulties, once raised, had to be discussed until they were solved.

In his last years Plotinus, whose health had never been very good, suffered from a painful and repulsive sickness that Porphyry describes so imprecisely that one modern scholar has identified it as tuberculosis and another as a form of leprosy. This made his friends, as he noticed, avoid his company, and he retired to a country estate belonging to one of them in Campania and within a year died there in the year 270. The circle of friends had already broken up. Plotinus himself had sent Porphyry away to Sicily to recover from his depression. Amelius was in Syria. Only his physician, Eustochius, arrived in time to be with Plotinus at the end.

KARL POPPER

(b. 1902– d. 1994)

Karl Raimund Popper was born in Vienna, Austria, on July 28, 1902. Originator of the theory of falsifiability, Karl Popper is best known for his rejection of the inductive method of reasoning in the empirical sciences. In inductive logic a statement of supposed fact—a hypothesis—is proven true if repeated observations substantiate it. In opposing this viewpoint, Popper insisted that hypotheses must be testable, and that the right test for a scientific hypothesis is to look for some circumstance for which it does not hold. If no such circumstance can be found, then the hypothesis is true.

He attended the University of Vienna, receiving his Ph.D. there in 1928. He taught in secondary schools in Vienna for a time, and then in 1937 he moved to New Zealand, where he taught philosophy at Canterbury University College until 1945. From 1945 until his retirement in 1969, he headed the department of philosophy, logic, and scientific method at the London School of Economics in England. He also lectured widely both in Great Britain and in the United States.

Popper's publications include a number of periodical articles and several books. In his first book, *The Logic of Scientific Discovery*, published in 1934, he presents his thoughts regarding falsifiability and inductive logic and outlines his method of distinguishing between sciences and pseudo-sciences. The theoretical constructs rejected by Popper as pseudo-sciences because they failed to pass his test of falsifiability include such fields of study as astrology, Freudian psychoanalysis, metaphysics, and Marxism.

Popper's later works include *The Open Society and Its Enemies* (1945) and *The Poverty of Historicism* (1957). In both of these books he opposes historical determinism, the view that history develops in accordance with inexorable natural laws. His three-volume *Postscript to the Logic of Scientific Discovery* (1981–82) expands on the ideas presented in his first book. Popper was knighted in 1965. He died in Croydon, Eng., on Sept. 17, 1994.

PYRRHON OF ELIS

(b. 360 BCE – d. c.272)

Pyrrhon of Elis was a Greek philosopher from whom Pyrrhonism takes its name. He is generally accepted as the father of Skepticism.

Pyrrhon was a pupil of Anaxarchus of Abdera and in about 330 established himself as a teacher at Elis. Believing that equal arguments can be offered on both sides of any proposition, he dismissed the search for truth as a vain endeavor. While traveling with an expedition under Alexander the Great, Pyrrhon saw in the fakirs of India an example of happiness flowing from indifference to circumstances. He concluded that man must suspend judgment (practice *epochē*) on the reliability of sense perceptions and simply live according to reality as it appears. Pyrrhonism permeated the Middle and New Academy of Athens and strongly influenced philosophical thought in 17th-century Europe with the republication of the Skeptical works of Sextus Empiricus, who had codified Greek Skepticism in the 3rd century CE. Pyrrhon's teaching was preserved in the poems of Timon of Phlius, who studied with him.

PYTHAGORAS

(b. 580? BCE – d. 500? BCE)

The man who played a crucial role in formulating principles that influenced Plato and Aristotle was the Greek philosopher and mathematician Pythagoras. He founded the Pythagorean brotherhood, a group of his followers whose beliefs and ideas were rediscovered during the Renaissance and contributed to the development of mathematics and Western rational philosophy.

Pythagoras was born in about 580 BCE on the island of Samos, in the Aegean Sea. It is said he spent his early years traveling widely in search of wisdom. He settled in Crotona, a Greek colony in southern Italy, about 530 BCE. A brotherhood of disciples soon gathered around him, inspired by his teachings. The group was strongly religious and devoted to reformation of political, moral, and social life. The order was influential in the region, but eventually its involvement in politics resulted in suppression of the brotherhood. Pythagoras was forced to retire and leave the area. He went to Metapontum, a Greek city in southern Italy. He died there in about 500 BCE.

Because none of the writings of Pythagoras has survived, it is difficult to distinguish his teachings from those of his disciples. Among the basic tenets of the Pythagoreans are the beliefs that reality, at its deepest level, is mathematical in nature; philosophy can be used for spiritual purification; and that the soul can rise to union with the divine. Pythagoras is generally credited with the theory of the functional significance of numbers in the objective world and in music. His followers are credited with the development of the Pythagorean theorem in geometry and the application of number relationships to music theory, acoustics, and astronomy.

Bust of Pythagoras, the Greek mathematician and philosopher whose principles guided the great Greek philosophers Aristotle and Plato. DEA/G Dagli Orti/De Agostini/Getty Images

WILLARD VAN ORMAN QUINE

(b. 1908 – d. 2000)

U.S. philosopher Willard Van Orman Quine was born on June 25, 1908, in Akron, Ohio. He specialized in language analysis and logic. Although his early career emphasized technical aspects of logic as a basis for philosophy, his later work investigated more general philosophical issues within a systematic linguistic framework.

Quine trained in mathematics at Oberlin College and then switched to philosophy at Harvard University, where he earned a doctorate in

1932. He later studied at Oxford and Prague. Quine taught at Harvard from 1936 to 1978. He also traveled extensively and lectured at schools throughout the world. He was honored as president of the American Philosophical Association (1951) and the Association for Symbolic Logic (1953–55) and received the Butler Gold Medal from Columbia University (1970) in addition to many honorary degrees. Among his publications are *A System of Logistic* (1934), *Mathematical Logic* (1940), *Elementary Logic* (1941), *From a Logical Point of View* (1953), *Word and Object* (1960), *Set Theory and Its Logic* (1963), *Philosophy of Logic* (1970), and *The Roots of Reference* (1973). Quine died on Dec. 25, 2000, in Boston, Mass.

RAMANUJA

(b. 1017?–d. 1137)

The Indian theologian Ramanuja is known mainly from legends. He was born in southern India in what is now the state of Tamil Nadu, supposedly in 1017, which would have made him 120 when he died at Srirangam in 1137. He was the most influential figure in the history of devotional Hinduism. He taught that God, the world, and the individual soul are three separate realities. It is the soul's duty to serve God, whom Ramanuja worshipped as Vishnu. This view is in total contrast to that of his predecessor Sankara, who taught that all reality—God, the world, and the soul—is one.

He studied theology under a follower of Sankara but soon rejected what he was learning. After having a vision of Vishnu, he instituted daily worship to the god. For 20 years he was a pilgrim, traveling around India teaching his philosophy. He then returned to Srirangam, the town where he had developed the teaching that worship of a personal god is an essential part of Hinduism, based on ancient writings called the Upanishads. In Srirangam, Ramanuja organized temple worship and reportedly founded 74 centers to spread his teachings.

Ramanuja's chief contribution to Hinduism was providing an intellectual basis for popular devotion, called *bhakti*. Since his day bhakti has remained the major force in all branches of Hinduism. The devotion he inspired soon made its way to northern India, where it had its greatest influence.

JOHN RAWLS

(b. 1921– d. 2002)

The U.S. philosopher John Rawls is widely regarded as the most important political thinker of the 20th century. In *A Theory of Justice* (1971), he tried to defend the democratic values of fairness, equality, and individual rights using the concept of a social contract, which had been largely neglected in philosophy since the 18th century.

Rawls imagined a situation in which a group of people are isolated from society and then caused to "forget" certain facts about themselves, such as facts about their sex, race, religion, education, wealth, intelligence, and talents or skills. They are then asked to decide what general rules or principles they would like their government to follow.

Because the members of the group do not know what position in society they occupy, they are compelled to choose principles that will ensure that they are treated fairly and that their rights are respected, no matter who they are or where they come from. Therefore, from behind this "veil of ignorance," they would choose principles like the following:

Photograph of U.S. philosopher John Rawls, taken in Paris in the 1980s. Frederic Reglain/Gammo-Rapho/ Getty Images

Everyone should have a maximum and equal degree of liberty.

Everyone should have an equal opportunity to pursue jobs, education, and other sources of wealth and power.

Inequality of wealth should be permitted, but only if those who are poorest are as well-off as they can be.

Rawls thought that some inequality of wealth was necessary in order to motivate people to be productive. The last principle means that whatever inequality of wealth there is should be the minimum necessary to make everyone as well-off as possible.

RICHARD RORTY

(b. 1931 – d. 2007)

Richard McKay Rorty was born on Oct. 4, 1931, in New York. He was an American pragmatist philosopher and public intellectual noted for his wide-ranging critique of the modern conception of philosophy as a quasi-scientific enterprise aimed at reaching certainty and objective truth. In politics he argued against programs of both the left and the right in favor of what he described as "bourgeois liberalism."

The son of nonacademic leftist intellectuals who broke with the American Communist Party in the early 1930s, Rorty attended the University of Chicago and Yale University, where he obtained a Ph.D. in 1956. Following two years in the army, he taught philosophy at Wellesley College (1958–61) and Princeton University (1961–82) before accepting a position in the department of humanities at the University of Virginia. From 1998 until his retirement in 2005, Rorty taught comparative literature at Stanford University.

Rorty's views are somewhat easier to characterize in negative than in positive terms. In epistemology he opposed foundationalism, the view that all knowledge can be grounded, or justified, in a set of basic statements that do not themselves require justification. According to his "epistemological behaviorism," Rorty held that no statement is epistemologically more basic than any other, and no statement is ever justified "finally" but only relative to some circumscribed and contextually determined set of additional statements. In the philosophy of language, Rorty rejected the idea that sentences or beliefs are "true" or "false" in any interesting sense other than being useful or successful within a broad social practice. He also opposed representationism, the view that the main function of language is to represent or picture pieces of an objectively existing reality. Finally, in metaphysics he rejected both realism and antirealism, or idealism, as products of mistaken representationalist assumptions about language.

Because Rorty did not believe in certainty or absolute truth, he did not advocate the philosophical pursuit of such things. Instead, he believed that the role of philosophy is to conduct an intellectual "conversation" between contrasting but equally valid forms of intellectual inquiry—including science, literature, politics, religion, and many others—with the aim of achieving mutual understanding and resolving conflicts. This general view is reflected in Rorty's political works, which consistently defend traditional left-liberalism and criticize newer forms of "cultural leftism" as well as more conservative positions.

Rorty defended himself against charges of relativism and subjectivism by claiming that he rejected the crucial distinctions these doctrines presuppose. Nevertheless, some critics have contended that his views lead ultimately to relativist or subjectivist conclusions, whether or not Rorty wished to characterize them in those terms. Others have challenged Rorty's interpretation of earlier American pragmatist philosophers and suggested that Rorty's own philosophy is not a genuine form of pragmatism.

Rorty's publications include *Philosophy and the Mirror of Nature* (1979), *Consequences of Pragmatism* (1982), and *Contingency, Irony, and Solidarity* (1989). Rorty died on June 8, 2007 in Palo Alto, Cali.

JEAN-JACQUES ROUSSEAU
(b. 1712– d. 1778)

The famous Swiss-born philosopher Jean-Jacques Rousseau gave better advice and followed it less than perhaps any other great man. Although he wrote glowingly about nature, he spent much time in crowded Paris. He praised married life and wrote wisely about the education of children, but he lived with his servant, marrying her only after 23 years, and gave up their babies. He taught hygiene, yet he lived in a stuffy garret. Rousseau himself was unable to guide his behavior to follow his beliefs. Yet his writings on politics, literature, and education have had a profound influence on modern thought.

Rousseau was born in Geneva, Switz., on June 28, 1712. He was of French Huguenot descent and his father was a watchmaker. Young Rousseau grew up undisciplined, and at about the age of 16 he became a vagabond. In Chambéry, France, he met and lived with Madame de Warens, a woman who was to influence his intellectual evolution. For a while he roamed through Switzerland, Italy, and France, earning his way as secretary, tutor, and music teacher. When he went to Paris in 1741, he was impressed by the fact that society was artificial and unfair in its organization.

This unknown wanderer upset that whole elaborate society. After years of thought Rousseau wrote a book on the origins of government, *The Social Contract*, stating that no laws are binding unless agreed upon by the people. This idea deeply affected French thinking, and it became one of the chief forces that brought on the French Revolution about 30 years later.

Rousseau helped bring about another revolution in education. In his novel *Émile* he assailed the way parents and teachers brought up and taught children. Rousseau urged that young people be given freedom to enjoy sunlight, exercise, and play. He recognized that there are definite periods of development in a child's life, and he argued that children's learning should be scheduled to coincide with them. A child allowed to grow up in this fashion will achieve the best possible development. Education should begin in the home. Parents should not preach to their children but should set a good example. Rousseau believed that children should make their own decisions.

In literature, too, Rousseau inspired a profound change. He stirred writers to realize that the beauties of nature have a rightful place in literature. The Romantic movement in Germany, France, and England owes much to Rousseau's influence and example. He dared to write of his most intimate emotions. His autobiographical *Confessions* is considered a masterpiece of self-revelation.

Rousseau was persecuted for his innovative ideas and fled France in 1762. For a time he lived in Switzerland and then with the historian David Hume in England. He later returned to France.

Careful readers of Rousseau find many flaws in his logic, especially in his greatest book, *The Social Contract*. Rousseau was broad-minded enough to realize that his was not the final word on government. Rousseau also Published *The New Héloïse* (1761); *and his Discourse on the Origin of Inequality*, published in 1755, was nearly as influential as *The Social Contract*. The *Confessions*, written in his later years, was published in 1782. Rousseau died in Ermenonville, near Paris, on July 2, 1778.

French philosopher Jean-Jacques Rousseau. Library of Congress Prints and Photographs Division

BERTRAND RUSSELL

(b. 1872– d. 1970)

Bertrand Arthur William Russell was born on May 18, 1872, at Trelleck in Monmouthshire, Eng. During his almost 98 years, Russell was a scholar in almost every field: philosophy, logic, mathematics, science, sociology, education, history, religion, and politics. He was a pacifist, an advocate of social justice, and a supporter of nuclear disarmament. Yet it was for literature that he won the Nobel Prize in 1950.

He was the author of several dozen books, many of them written for a general audience.

He was the second son of Viscount Amberley, a title to which he succeeded in 1931 after his brother Frank's death. His parents died when he was quite young, so he was brought up by his paternal grandmother. He was educated privately in his early years before entering Trinity College, Cambridge. He took mathematics honors in 1893 and graduated in 1894. For two years Russell lectured in the United States before returning home to a lectureship at the London School of Economics.

One of his goals was to prove that mathematics could be derived from self-evident principles. His first attempt to do so was in *The Principles of Mathematics* published in 1903. Ten years later the task was advanced with *Principia Mathematica* (1910–13), written with Alfred North Whitehead. Russell received a teaching appointment at Trinity College in 1910 but lost it in 1916 because of his pacifism. He was also jailed for six months in 1918. While in prison he wrote *Introduction to Mathematical Philosophy* (1919). Russell visited the Soviet Union in 1920 and afterward wrote a highly critical book, *The Practice and Theory of Bolshevism* (1920). During the next 12 years he published a number of other popular books, including *What I Believe* (1925), *Why I Am Not a Christian* (1927), and *Marriage and Morals* (1929). His philosophical speculations on the nature of knowledge were published as *Human Knowledge, Its Scope and Limits* (1948).

Post World War II Russell turned his attention to international politics. He encouraged civil disobedience and sit-ins to protest nuclear weapons. In the 1960s he protested American involvement in Vietnam. The Bertrand Russell Peace Foundation was established by him in 1963. The last three years of his life were devoted to writing his autobiography. He died in Merioneth, Wales, on Feb. 2, 1970.

JEAN-PAUL SARTRE

(b. 1905–d. 1980)

Jean-Paul Sartre was born on June 21, 1905, in Paris, France. One of the leading formulators of existentialism, Jean-Paul Sartre was also well known as a writer. He expressed his dedication to his philosophy both in what he wrote and in the way he lived his life.

In 1919 he graduated from the École Normale Supérieure, where he met his lifelong companion, the writer Simone de Beauvoir. Between 1931 and 1945 he taught at several secondary schools in France. During the 1930s he began to develop his existentialist philosophy, which stressed personal freedom and stated that the individual exists only in relation to other people. In 1938 he published his first major work, the novel *Nausea*, in which he set these ideas in writing.

In 1939 Sartre was drafted to serve in World War II. He was captured and placed in a prisoner-of-war camp in 1940, but he escaped the following year and returned to Paris, where he became active in the Resistance. After the war Sartre became a celebrity. His writings began to focus on the necessity for action, or doing, rather than simply existing. This led to an increased commitment to politics. In 1945 Sartre cofounded with de Beauvoir a monthly review of politics, philosophy, and art called *Les Temps Modernes*. In 1952 Sartre allied himself with the French Communist party, though he never actually became a member.

Sartre supported the student uprisings of May 1968, and he protested the United States involvement in Vietnam in the 1960s. In 1964 Sartre published his autobiography, entitled *Words*. He was awarded the 1964 Nobel Prize for literature but declined the prize. Some of the most significant of Sartre's works include the philosophical treatise *Being and Nothingness* (1943), the play *No Exit* (1945), and the short story *The Wall* (1939). Sartre died on April 15, 1980, in Paris.

ARTHUR SCHOPENHAUER
(b. 1788–d. 1860)

Arthur Schopenhauer was born in Danzig, Prussia (now Gdańsk, Pol.), on Feb. 22, 1788. Along with Friedrich Nietzsche, Schopenhauer was one of the great pessimists of 19th-century German philosophy. He had much to be pessimistic about. For most of his life he met the "resistance of a dull world," which took the form of indifference to his work. He was continually overshadowed by his philosophical foe, Georg

Wilhelm Friedrich Hegel. Not until a few years before his death did international acclaim come to Schopenhauer. He eventually had a deep influence on modern existentialism, psychology, philosophy of history, and literature.

He attended the universities of Göttingen and Berlin before receiving a doctorate from the University of Jena in 1813. He spent a year in Weimar with the poet Johann Wolfgang von Goethe working on the latter's theory of colors. He then settled in Dresden to finish his masterpiece, *The World as Will and Idea*, published in 1819. In 1820 he began to lecture at the University of Berlin but because he scheduled his lectures for the same hour during which Hegel lectured, he could gather no following. Frustrated that his book received no notice, he settled in Frankfurt am Main. He remained there, in relative seclusion, for the rest of his life.

Though initially overshadowed by his countryman Friedrich Hegel, German philosopher Arthur Schopenhauer eventually received a measure of international fame for his work. Hulton Archive/Getty Images

Schopenhauer continued writing. He produced *On the Will in Nature* (1836), *On the Freedom of the Will, and On the Basis of Morality* (1841), and a second edition of his main work. Then, with the publication in 1851 of two volumes of essays under the title *Parerga and Paralipomena* (literally, *Minor Works and Remnants*), he began to attract international attention. The publication in England of an attack on Hegel's philosophy led to the appearance of favorable treatises on Schopenhauer's work. Translations of his books were made, and he was praised throughout Europe. Amid the prevailing

Romanticism of the time his emphasis on vitalism, intuition, creativity, and the irrational found a warm reception. He spent his last years revising his books. He died suddenly in Frankfurt on Sept. 21, 1860.

JOHN DUNS SCOTUS
(b. 1265?–d. 1308)

John Duns Scotus was a Scottish theologian and philosopher. He was also known as Doctor Subtilis. He was born at Duns, and is regarded as one of the greatest of the scholastics. Scotus was a celebrated opponent of doctrines of Thomas Aquinas. Scotus and his followers took up the name "Duns men." This gave rise to use of his name in the form of "dunce" to mean pedant and, later, ignoramus.

WILFRID SELLARS
(b. 1912–d. 1989)

Wilfrid Stalker Sellars was born on May 20, 1912, in Ann Arbor, Mich., U.S.A. He is best known for his critique of traditional philosophical conceptions of mind and knowledge and for his uncompromising effort to explain how human reason and thought can be reconciled with the vision of nature found inscience. Although he was one of the most original and influential American philosophers of the second half of the 20th century, Sellars remains largely unknown outside academic circles.

Sellars's father, Roy Sellars, was a distinguished Canadian philosopher. After studying at the University of Michigan and the University of Buffalo, the younger Sellars was awarded a Rhodes scholarship to the University of Oxford, where he earned bachelor's (1936) and master's (1940) degrees in philosophy, politics, and economics. He was appointed assistant professor of philosophy at the University of Iowa in 1938. After serving as an intelligence officer in the U.S. Navy (1943–46), he was appointed assistant professor of philosophy at the University of Minnesota. He was professor of philosophy at Yale University from 1959 to 1963 and university professor of philosophy and research professor of philosophy at the University of Pittsburgh from 1963 until his death.

Sellars came to prominence in 1956 with the publication of his work *Empiricism and the Philosophy of Mind*, a critique of a conception of mind and knowledge inherited from René Descartes (1596–1650). Sellars there attacked what he called the "myth of the given," the Cartesian idea that one can have immediate and indubitable perceptual knowledge of one's own sense experiences. Sellars's ideas anticipated and contributed to the development of theories of mind, knowledge, and science that played significant roles in later debates on these topics.

Sellars was an articulate exponent of the modernist enterprise of reconciling the comprehensive picture of reality emerging from the theoretical activities of natural science with the traditional conception of human beings as morally accountable agents and subjective centers of experience. In *Philosophy and the Scientific Image of Man* (1960), he characterized this project as bringing together into one "synoptic view" two competing images of "man-in-the-world": the "scientific" image derived from the fruits of theory construction and the "manifest" image, the "framework in terms of which man encountered himself."

Sellars subscribed to a form of philosophical naturalism according to which science is the final arbiter of what exists. Entities exist if and only if they would be invoked in a complete scientific explanation of the world. In *Empiricism and the Philosophy of Mind*, he wrote, "In the dimension of describing and explaining the world, science is the measure of all things, of what is that it is, and of what is not that it is not." His synoptic project, however, required him to develop ways of accommodating dimensions of human experience that seem initially to resist incorporation into the "scientific image." Science describes how humans do think and act, for example, but not how they ought to think and act, and this latter element therefore requires explanation if it is to be reconciled with Sellars's naturalism. His fundamental response to these challenges was to develop a sophisticated theory of conceptual roles, concretely instantiated in human conduct and transmitted by modes of social interaction, including language. He used this theory in turn to defend a form of linguistic nominalism, the denial of the real existence of universals or irreducibly mentalistic entities as the referents or meanings of linguistic expressions. Sellars analyzed discourse about abstract or mentalistic entities as discourse about linguistic role players framed in a "transposed mode of speech."

Sellars's account of knowledge and experience drew upon his deep reading of the history of philosophy, particularly the works of Immanuel Kant (1724–1804). In contrast to at least some other advocates of naturalism, Sellars rejected the idea that normative concepts such as knowledge can or should be analyzed in terms of non-normative concepts. On Sellars's view, characterizing people as knowers does not require attributing to them a special inner psychological state but merely involves noting their ability to engage in various public behaviors, such as giving reasons for what they claim to know. Like Kant, he understood perceptual experience as synthesizing the contributions of a non-cognitive faculty of sensation and a conceptual faculty of thought.

Sellars is often credited with originating the theory of functionalism in the philosophy of mind, according to which mental states are individuated by the inferential roles they play in thought. Because functional states are independent of their physical realization, it is a consequence of Sellars's view that they can in principle be realized in digital computers as well as in biological organisms. But Sellars also argued that the classification of sensory mental states rests on analogies that ultimately pertain to similarities and differences of intrinsic content within those states. Sensations can therefore be synoptically integrated into the scientific image, he concluded, only after they and the microphysical details of the scientific image have been reconceived in terms of a uniform ontology whose fundamental entities are "absolute processes."

Sellars also introduced the functionalist idea of explaining semantic meaning in terms of the inferential and ultimately behavioral roles played by particular linguistic expressions, a view later known as conceptual-role semantics. Public speech episodes—i.e., particular linguistic utterances or acts of inscription—instantiate semantic-conceptual roles by virtue of being regulated by rules governing linguistic responses to non-conceptual stimuli ("language entries"), behavioral responses to conceptual states ("language exits"), and transitions from one linguistic commitment to another ("intra-linguistic moves"). Roles or functions are themselves individuated in terms of the structure of positive and negative uniformities generated in the natural order by such entries, exits, and moves.

Finally, Sellars proposed that what makes an entity a person is its membership in a community whose most general common intentions fundamentally define the structure of norms and values in terms of which the cognitive and moral conduct of those members comes to be mutually recognized and appraised. He consequently concluded that only by enriching the scientific image with a functionally interpreted language of intentions can one complete "the task of showing that categories pertaining to man as a person who finds himself confronted by standards...can be reconciled with the idea that man is what science says he is."

Sellars's major published works, in addition to the those mentioned above, include *Science, Perception, and Reality* (1963), *Philosophical Perspectives* (1967), *Science and Metaphysics: Variations on Kantian Themes* (1968), *Naturalism and Ontology* (1979), and *Foundations for a Metaphysics of Pure Process* (1981).

Sellars died on July 2, 1989, in Pitt., Pa.

SEXTUS EMPIRICUS

(fl. 3rd century)

Sextus Empiricus was an ancient Greek philosopher-historian who produced the only extant comprehensive account of Greek Skepticism in his *Outlines of Pyrrhonism* and *Against the Mathematicians.*

As a major exponent of Pyrrhonistic "suspension of judgment," Sextus elaborated the 10 tropes of Aenesidemus and attacked syllogistic proofs in every area of speculative knowledge. Almost all details of his life are conjectural except that he was a medical doctor and headed a Skeptical school during the decline of Greek Skepticism. The first printing of his *Outlines* in 1562 had far-reaching effects on European philosophical thought. Indeed, much of the philosophy of the 17th and

18th centuries can be interpreted in terms of diverse efforts to grapple with the ancient Skeptical arguments handed down through Sextus.

SHANKARA

(b. 700?– d. 750?)

Shankara, also called Shankaracharya, was a philosopher and theologian and the most renowned exponent of the Advaita Vedanta school of philosophy, from whose doctrines the main currents of modern Indian thought are derived. He wrote commentaries on the *Brahma-sutra*, the principal Upanishads, and the *Bhagavad-Gita*, affirming his belief in one eternal unchanging reality (Brahman) and the illusion of plurality and differentiation.

There are at least 11 works that profess to be biographies of Shankara. His date of birth is naturally a controversial problem. It was once customary to assign him the birth and death dates 788–820, but the dates 700–750, grounded in modern scholarship, are more acceptable.

According to one tradition, Shankara was born into a Nambudiri Brahman family in a quiet village called Kaladi on the Periyar (Purna) River, in Kerala in southern India. He is said to have lost his father, Shivaguru, early in his life. He renounced the world and became a *sannyasin* (ascetic) against his mother's will. He studied under Govinda, who was a pupil of Gaudapada. Nothing certain is known about Govinda, but Gaudapada is notable as the author of an important Vedanta work, *Mandukya-karika*, in which the influence of Mahayana Buddhism—a form of Buddhism aiming at the salvation of all beings and tending toward non-dualistic or monistic thought—is evident and even extreme, especially in its last chapter.

Biographers narrate that Shankara first went to Kashi (Varanasi), a city celebrated for learning and spirituality, and then traveled all over India, holding discussions with philosophers of different creeds. His heated debate with Mandana Mishra, a philosopher of the Mimamsa (Investigation) school, whose wife served as an umpire, is perhaps the most interesting episode in his biography and may reflect a historical fact—that is, keen conflict between Shankara, who regarded the knowledge of

Artist portrayal of Indian philosopher Shankara, whose doctrines heavily influenced modern Indian thought. Godong/Universal Images Group/ Getty Images

brahman as the only means to final release, and followers of the Mimamsa school, which emphasized the performance of ordained duty and the Vedic rituals.

Shankara was active in a politically chaotic age. He would not teach his doctrine to city dwellers. The power of Buddhism was still strong in the cities, though already declining, and Jainism, a nontheistic ascetic faith, prevailed among the merchants and manufacturers. Popular Hinduism occupied the minds of ordinary people, while city dwellers pursued ease and pleasure. There were also epicureans in cities. It was difficult for Shankara to communicate Vedanta philosophy to these people. Consequently, Shankara propagated his teachings chiefly to sannyasins and intellectuals in the villages, and he gradually won the respect of Brahmans and feudal lords.

It is very likely that Shankara had many pupils, but only four are known (from their writings): Padmapada, Sureshvara, Totaka (or Trotaka), and Hastamalaka. Shankara is said to have founded four monasteries, at Shringeri (south), Puri (east), Dvaraka (west), and Badarinatha (north), probably following the Buddhist monastery (vihara) system. Their foundation was one of the most significant factors in the development of his teachings into the leading philosophy of India.

More than 300 works—commentative, expository, and poetical—written in the Sanskrit language are attributed to him. Most of them, however, cannot be regarded as authentic. His masterpiece is the

Brahma-sutra-bhashya, the commentary on the *Brahma-sutra*, which is a fundamental text of the Vedanta school. The commentary on the *Mandukya-karika* was also composed by Shankara himself. It is very probable that he is the author of the *Yoga-sutra-bhashya-vivarana*, the exposition of Vyasa's commentary on the *Yoga-sutra*, a fundamental text of the Yoga school. The *Upadeshasahasri*, which is a good introduction to Shankara's philosophy, is the only non-commentative work that is certainly authentic.

Shankara's style of writing is lucid and profound. Penetrating insight and analytical skill characterize his works. His approach to truth is psychological and religious rather than logical and for that reason, he is perhaps best considered to be a prominent religious teacher rather than a philosopher in the modern sense. His works reveal that he not only was versed in the orthodox Brahmanical traditions but also was well acquainted with Mahayana Buddhism. He is often criticized as a "Buddhist in disguise" by his opponents because of the similarity between his doctrine and Buddhism. Despite this criticism, it should be noted that he made full use of his knowledge of Buddhism to attack Buddhist doctrines severely or to transmute them into his own Vedantic nondualism, and he tried with great effort to "vedanticize" the Vedanta philosophy, which had been made extremely Buddhistic by his predecessors. The basic structure of his philosophy is more akin to Samkhya, a philosophic system of nontheistic dualism, and the Yoga school than to Buddhism. It is said that Shankara died at Kedarnatha in the Himalayas. The Advaita Vedanta School founded by him has always been preeminent in the learned circles of India.

SHINRAN

(b. 1173 – d. 1262)

Shinran was a Japanese philosopher and religious reformer. Shinran founded the Jodo Shinsa (True Pure Land sect), the largest sect of Buddhism in Japan today. He studied Buddhism for 20 years on Mount Hiei, and then became a follower of Honen, the founder of the Pure Land sect. From 1212 to 1236 Shinran lived at Kanto in eastern Japan, where he wrote *Teaching-Acting-Faith-Attainment*. He taught a belief in justification by faith alone that has been compared to the thought of Martin Luther. Shinran died in Kyoto in 1262.

PETER SINGER

(b. 1946-)

Peter Albert David Singer was born on July 6, 1946, in Melbourne, Australia. He is an Australian ethical and political philosopher, best known for his work in bioethics and his role as one of the intellectual founders of the modern animal rights movement.

Singer's Jewish parents immigrated to Australia from Vienna in 1938 to escape Nazi persecution following the Anschluss. Three of Singer's grandparents were later killed in the Holocaust. Growing up in Melbourne, Singer attended Scotch College and the University of Melbourne, where he earned a B. A. in philosophy and history (1967) and an M.A. in philosophy (1969). In 1969 he entered the University of Oxford, receiving a B. Phil. degree in 1971 and serving as Radcliffe Lecturer in Philosophy at University College from 1971 to 1973. At Oxford his association with a vegetarian student group and his reflection on the morality of his own meat eating led him to adopt vegetarianism. While at Oxford and during a visiting professorship at New York University in 1973–74, he wrote what would become his best-known and most influential work, *Animal Liberation: A New Ethics for Our Treatment of Animals* (1975). Returning to Australia, he lectured at La Trobe University (1975–76) and was appointed professor of philosophy at Monash University (1977); he became director of Monash's Centre for Human Bioethics in 1983 and co-director of its Institute for Ethics and Public Policy in 1992. In 1999 he was appointed Ira W. DeCamp Professor of Bioethics in the University Center for Human Values at Princeton University.

In keeping with ethical principles that guided his thinking and writing from the 1970s, Singer devoted much of his time and effort (and a considerable portion of his income) to social and political causes, most notably animal rights but also famine and poverty relief, environmentalism, and reproductive rights. By the 1990s his intellectual leadership of the increasingly successful animal rights movement and his controversial stands on some bioethical issues had made him one of the world's most widely recognized public intellectuals.

Singer's work in applied ethics and his activism in politics were informed by his utilitarianism, the tradition in ethical philosophy that holds that actions are right or wrong depending on the extent to which they promote happiness or prevent pain. In an influential early article, "Famine, Affluence, and Morality" (1972), occasioned by the catastrophic cyclone in Bangladesh in 1971, he rejected the common pre-philosophical assumption that physical proximity is a relevant factor in determining one's moral obligations to others. Regarding the question of whether people in affluent countries have a greater obligation to help those near them than to contribute to famine relief in Bangladesh, he wrote: "It makes no moral difference whether the person I can help is a neighbor's child ten yards from me or a Bengali whose name I shall never know, ten thousand miles away." The only important question, according to Singer, is whether the evil that may be prevented by one's contribution outweighs whatever inconvenience or hardship may be involved in contributing—and for the large majority of people in affluent societies, the answer is clearly yes.

An interesting philosophical implication of Singer's larger argument was that the traditional distinction between duty and charity—between actions that one is obliged to do and actions that it would be good to do even though one is not obliged to do them—was seriously weakened, if not completely undermined. On the utilitarian principles Singer plausibly applied to this case, any action becomes a duty if it will prevent more pain than it causes or cause more happiness than it prevents.

The publication of *Animal Liberation* in 1975 greatly contributed to the growth of the animal rights movement by calling attention to the routine torture and abuse of countless animals in factory farms and in scientific research; at the same time, it generated significant new interest among ethical philosophers in the moral status of nonhuman animals. The most important philosophical contribution of the book was Singer's penetrating examination of the concept of "speciesism" (which he did not invent): the idea that the species membership of a being should be relevant to its moral status. To the contrary, argued Singer, all beings

113

with interests (all beings who are capable of enjoyment or suffering, broadly construed) deserve to have those interests taken into account in any moral decision making that affects them; furthermore, the kind of consideration a being deserves should depend on the nature of the interests it has (what kinds of enjoyment or suffering it is capable of), not on the species it happens to belong to. To think otherwise is to endorse a prejudice exactly analogous to racism or sexism. Speciesism was extensively explored by ethical philosophers and eventually became a familiar theme in popular discussions of animal rights in a variety of forums.

In numerous books and articles published in the 1980s and after, Singer continued to develop his positions on animal rights and other topics in applied ethical and political philosophy—including stem cell research, infanticide, euthanasia, global environmental concerns, and the political implications of Darwinism, placing them within the context of theoretical developments in utilitarianism. Even as his philosophical defense of animal rights gained currency in academia and beyond, however, his stances on other issues engendered new controversies, some of which pitted him against people who had supported his work on behalf of animal rights or had been sympathetic to his general philosophical approach. In 1999, his appointment to Princeton University was protested by activists on behalf of the disabled, who objected to his view that the active euthanasia of severely disabled human infants is morally permissible in some circumstances.

In addition to *Animal Liberation*, Singer's many books include *Practical Ethics* (1979), *Rethinking Life and Death: The Collapse of Our Traditional Ethics* (1994), *A Darwinian Left* (1999), and *One World: Ethics and Globalization* (2002). Singer is also the author of Encyclopedia Britannica's article on ethics.

SOCRATES

(b. 470? BCE–d. 399 BCE)

Interested in neither money, nor fame, nor power, Socrates wandered the streets of Athens in the 5th century BCE. He wore a single rough woolen garment in all seasons and went barefoot. Talking to whoever would listen, he asked questions, criticized answers, and poked holes in faulty arguments. His style of conversation has been given the name "Socratic dialogue."

Socrates was the wisest philosopher of his time. He was the first of the three great teachers of ancient Greece—the other two being Plato and Aristotle. Today he is ranked as one of the world's greatest moral teachers. In appearance he was short and fat, with a snub nose and wide mouth. Despite his appearance, the Greeks of his day enjoyed talking with him and were fascinated by what he had to say. The young, aristocratic military genius Alcibiades said of him, "His nature is so beautiful, golden, divine, and wonderful within that everything he commands surely ought to be obeyed even like the voice of a god."

Socrates was born on the outskirts of Athens in about 470 BCE. He studied sculpture, his father's profession, but soon abandoned this work to "seek truth" in his own way. His habits were so frugal and his constitution so hardy that he needed only the bare necessities. Although Socrates took no part in the politics of Athens, he would perform civic functions when he was called upon. He was a courageous soldier. During the Peloponnesian War he served as a foot soldier in several engagements. At Potidaea he saved the life of Alcibiades.

Statue of Socrates, the first of the great philosophers of ancient Greece, outside the national academy in Athens. Anastasios71/Shutterstock.com

Socrates' wife, Xanthippe, was notorious in Athens for her sharp tongue and quick temper. The sage once jokingly said, "As I intended to associate with all kinds of people, I thought nothing they could do would disturb me, once I had accustomed myself to bear the disposition of Xanthippe."

Socrates shunned the shallow notion of truth for its own sake. He turned to his conscience for moral truth and enjoyed creating confusion by asking simple questions. He sought to uncover the nature of virtue and to find a rule of life. Favorite objects of his attacks were the Sophists, who charged a fee for their teaching. "Know thyself" was the motto he is reputed to have learned from the oracle at Delphi. In knowing oneself he saw the possibility of learning what is really good, in contrast to accepting only outward appearance.

Socrates did not write any books or papers. The details of his life and doctrine are preserved in the *Memorabilia* of the historian Xenophon and in the dialogues of the philosopher Plato. It was mainly through Plato and Plato's brilliant disciple Aristotle that the influence of Socrates was passed on to succeeding generations of philosophers.

Socrates, however, was not appreciated by the Athenian mob and its self-serving leaders. His genius for exposing pompous frauds made him many enemies. At last, three of his political foes indicted him on the charge of "neglect of the gods" and "corruption of the young." They were false charges, but politically convenient. He was sentenced to die by drinking hemlock. His parting comments to his judges were simple, as recorded in Plato's *Apology*: "The hour of departure has arrived, and we go our ways—I to die, and you to live. Which is better God only knows."

HERBERT SPENCER

(b. 1820 – d. 1903)

Herbert Spencer was born in Derby, Eng., on April 27, 1820, where his father was a schoolmaster. It was Spencer, not Charles Darwin, who coined the phrase "survival of the fittest." Although Spencer's development of a theory of evolution preceded publication of

Darwin's *Origin of Species*, Spencer is today regarded as one of the leading social Darwinists of the 19th century. The theory, based on Darwin's conclusions, suggests that people and societies are subject to the same laws of natural selection as plants and animals are in nature.

Spencer is remembered today as author of *Social Statics* (1851), in which he argued that it is the business of government to uphold and defend natural rights. Beyond this, government should not interfere with the economic functioning of society at all. He saw his main task as developing a philosophy that would link the principles of many areas of knowledge to replace the theological systems of the Middle Ages. His work *The Synthetic Philosophy* was published in several volumes from 1862 to 1896.

He declined an offer to attend Cambridge University. Most of his higher education came through reading. He taught school for a few months, and from 1837 to 1841 he was a railway engineer. In 1842 he contributed a series of letters to a magazine, *The Nonconformist*. These letters were later published as *The Proper Sphere of Government*. He worked in various journalistic positions until 1848, when he became an editor of *The Economist*. He published *The Principles of Psychology* in 1855. Other books, apart from those included in his synthesis, are *The Study of Sociology* (1872), *The Man Versus the State* (1884), and his posthumous *Autobiography* (1904).

Spencer was one of the most opinionated and argumentative English thinkers of his time. He was a friend of such other writers as George Eliot (Mary Ann Evans), Thomas Henry Huxley, John Stuart Mill, and Beatrice Webb. Webb recorded Spencer's last years in her work, *My Apprenticeship* (1926). Spencer died in Brighton on Dec. 8, 1903.

BENEDICT DE SPINOZA
(b. 1632 – d. 1677)

Benedict de Spinoza was born on Nov. 24, 1632, in Amsterdam. He was a Dutch Jewish philosopher, one of the foremost exponents of 17th-century Rationalism and one of the early and essential figures of the Enlightenment.

Spinoza's Portuguese parents were among many Jews who were forcibly converted to Christianity but continued to practice Judaism in secret. After being arrested, tortured, and condemned by the inquisition in Portugal, they facilitated his escape to Amsterdam. The community there developed many social and educational institutions, including an all-male Talmud-Torah school founded in 1638. As a student in this school, the young Baruch Spinoza probably learned Hebrew and studied some Jewish philosophy, including that of Moses Maimonides.

In 1655 a book titled *Prae-Adamitae* (Latin: "Men Before Adam"), by the French courtier Isaac La Peyrère, appeared in Amsterdam. It challenged the accuracy of the Bible and insisted that the spread of human beings to all parts of the globe implies that there must have been humans before Adam and Eve. Spinoza owned a copy of the work, and many of La Peyrère's ideas about the Bible later appeared in Spinoza's writings.

La Peyrère's heresies may well have been the starting point of Spinoza's falling out with the synagogue in Amsterdam. In the summer of 1656 he was formally excommunicated. Sometime after his excommunication, he changed his given name from the Hebrew Baruch to the Latin Benedictus, both of which mean "blessed. " Ultimately, however, his excommunication may have had more to do with the presentation rather than the content of his beliefs.

In 1661 Spinoza moved from Amsterdam to the coastal town of Rijnsburg. Spinoza noted that he left Amsterdam because someone had tried to kill him with a knife as he emerged from a theatre. (He kept the coat he had been wearing, torn by the knife, for the rest of his life.) In Rijnsburg Spinoza lived alone in a modest but comfortable cottage, where he worked on his philosophy and supported himself by grinding lenses.

In 1661 Spinoza began writing the *Tractatus de Intellectus Emendatione* (*Treatise on the Emendation of the Intellect*), a presentation of his theory of knowledge, which he left unfinished. In about 1662 he completed his only work in Dutch, *Korte verhandeling van God, de mensch en deszelfs welstand* (*Short Treatise on God, Man and His Well-Being*), a brief survey of his overall philosophy. During this period he was also working on the *Ethics*, as his correspondence shows.

In 1663 Spinoza published *Renati des Cartes Principiorum Philosophiae* (1663; *René Descartes Principles of Philosophy*), the only one of his works to be published under his own name in his lifetime. An exposition of Descartes's *Principia Philosophiae* (1644; *Principles of Philosophy*), it showed a profound understanding of Descartes's system.

In the mid-1660s Spinoza moved again, to the outskirts of The Hague, where he spent the rest of his life. He began to acquire a wide circle of intellectual acquaintances. The publication of the *Tractatus Theologico-Politicus* in 1670 made Spinoza notorious. Although his name did not appear on the work, he was quickly known as its author. The *Tractatus* was one of the few books to be officially banned in the Netherlands during this period, though it could be bought easily. It was soon the topic of heated discussion throughout Europe.

The *Tractatus's* early chapters can be seen as the culmination of Spinoza's long-standing skepticism regarding the Bible. The first seven chapters in particular contain many borrowings from La Peyrère's *Prae-Adamitae* and from *Book III of Leviathan* (1651), by the English philosopher (and atheist) Thomas Hobbes. Although most of the discussion concerns Judaism and the Hebrew Bible (Old Testament), Spinoza also briefly indicates that Christian ceremonial law is also historically determined and therefore not binding on the modern believer. He cites in support of his conclusion the fact that Dutch Christians in Japan were willing to set aside all of their religious paraphernalia and practice during their trading visits in the country. At the end of the *Tractatus*, Spinoza argues for complete freedom of thought and of speech. People should be allowed to say and publish whatever they wish, so long as it does not interfere with the state.

Spinoza resumed work on his masterpiece, the *Ethica* (*Ethics*), finishing a five-part version by 1675. He delayed its publication, however, after being advised that it would cause even greater controversy than the *Tractatus*.

Ethica was finally published, together with the *Treatise on the Emendation of the Intellect* and an unfinished work on politics, the *Tractatus Politicus*, at the instigation of some of his Collegiant friends a few months after his death from consumption in 1677.

SAINT THOMAS AQUINAS

(b. 1225?– d. 1274)

The Roman Catholic Church regards St. Thomas Aquinas as its greatest theologian and philosopher. Pope John XXII canonized him in 1323, and Pius V declared him a Doctor of the Church in 1567. Leo XIII made him patron of Roman Catholic schools in 1880.

Thomas Aquinas, or Thomas of Aquino, was born in about 1225 in the castle of Roccasecca, near Naples. His father was the count of Aquino. The boy received his early education at the abbey of Monte Cassino before attending the University of Naples. While at the university Thomas came under the influence of the Dominicans, an order of mendicant preaching friars. In spite of the opposition of his family, he joined the order. His brothers captured him and imprisoned him at Roccasecca. After two years he escaped.

The Dominicans then sent Thomas to Cologne to study with Albertus Magnus, the most learned man of the time. In 1252 Thomas was in Paris composing his Commentaries on the Books of Sentences of Peter the Lombard. He was later admitted as master of theology at the University of Paris.

In 1259 the Pope called Thomas to Rome. He spent the rest of his life lecturing and preaching in the service of his order, chiefly in Italian cities and in Paris. A revival of learning had begun in Western Europe toward the end of the 11th century. By the 13th century many universities had been founded. They were linked to the church, and the chief subjects taught were theology and the liberal arts. The teachers were called Schoolmen or Scholastics. Thomas was recognized in his lifetime as the greatest of the Schoolmen and was known as the "angelic doctor."

The Schoolmen accepted Christian doctrines as beyond dispute, but they also studied the ancient Greek philosophers. Until the 13th century they relied on Plato as interpreted by St. Augustine of Hippo. Aristotle's treatises on logic were also admitted into the schools, but his other works, which were known in their Arabic translations, were forbidden because of their pan-theistic tendencies. Albertus Magnus introduced Thomas to the works of Aristotle, which were beginning to be trans-lated from the original Greek. Thomas set himself the task of harmonizing Aristotle's teach-ings with Christian doctrine. Thomas held that there are two sources of knowledge: revelation (theology) and rea-son (philosophy). He held that revelation is a divine source of knowledge and that revealed truths must be believed even when they cannot be fully understood. His literary out-put was enormous. At times he dictated to several scribes on different subjects. His

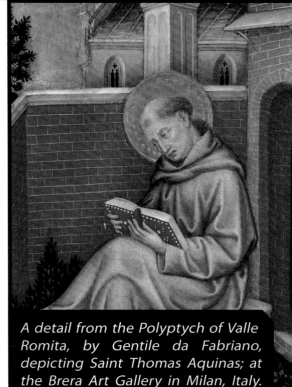

A detail from the Polyptych of Valle Romita, by Gentile da Fabriano, depicting Saint Thomas Aquinas; at the Brera Art Gallery in Milan, Italy. Mondadori Portfolio/Getty Images

chief works are *Summa contra gentiles* and *Summa theologiae*, which form the classical systematization of Roman Catholic theology.

He died on March 7, 1274, while traveling to a church council at Lyons.

GIANBATTISTA VICO

(b. 1668–d. 1744)

Gianbattista Vico was born in Naples, Italy, on June 23, 1668, to a poor family. A major figure in European intellectual history, Vico influenced the writings of such notable thinkers as Goethe, Auguste Comte, and Karl Marx. In his *New Science*, published in 1725, he devel-oped a remarkable philosophy of history.

Human societies, he claimed, pass through predictable stages of growth and decay. They go from a "bestial" state, in which they are ruled by superstition, and then they stabilize and divide into classes. Class conflict follows, in which the lower classes attain equal rights. This leads to corruption, dissolution, and sometimes a return to the bestial condition as security and money become life's goals.

He had some schooling but was mostly self-educated. He was professor of rhetoric at the University of Naples from 1699 until his death there on Jan. 23, 1744. During his lifetime Vico sought in vain to have his ideas read and considered. But it was only in the decades after his death that they began to gain notice. Goethe praised the *New Science* for its "prophetic insights based on sober meditation about life and about the future." Marx's economic interpretation of history owes a good deal to Vico. Many scholars now see Vico as an early thinker on anthropology and ethnology because of his insightful views on human nature.

WANG YANGMING
(b. 1472– d. 1529)

W ang Yangming was born in Yuyao, Zhejiang Province, in 1472, the son of a high government official. Chinese scholar-official Wang Yangming was a Neo-Confucianist philosopher who opposed the prevailing philosophical view in China in the 16th century. That view was another branch of Neo-Confucianism, known as the School of Principle. It was dominated by the work of the 12th-century rationalist Zhu Xi, whose philosophy centered on the study of the nature of things. By contrast, Wang Yangming emphasized inner reflection as the way to perfect the mind and understand the world. His thought was in the tradition known as the School of the Mind. Wang influenced philosophical thinking in East Asia for centuries, and he is regarded as one of the greatest Chinese thinkers of the last 2,000 years.

After obtaining a civil service degree, he twice failed the civil service examination before passing it in 1499. He was then appointed to the Ministry of Works. Wang's talents as an innovator in government earned him early recognition, and by 1504 he had become a secretary in the Ministry of War.

Despite personal misfortune, Wang developed some of his most important doctrines during the first decade of the 16th century. In 1506 he was whipped, imprisoned, and then banished to remote Guizhou Province for speaking out against a corrupt official. The hardships of his banishment led him to realize that the proper way to investigate the underlying principles (*li*) of things is not to seek for them in external objects, as Zhu Xi had taught, but in one's own mind.

The Confucian tradition had always emphasized that knowledge and action should correspond, but Wang went further, claiming that "knowledge is the beginning of action and action the completion of knowledge." Thus, one fully knows something—filial devotion, for example—only when one acts upon it. Wang described his theory as the "medicine" that would prevent people from avoiding action because they think they lack the necessary knowledge.

Wang's account of the human mind drew upon the Confucian text known as the *Daxue* (*Great Learning*) as well as the sage Mencius's idea that the mind has innate knowledge of the good. Wang believed that the mind's innate knowledge may be corrupted by thoughts and the will but its original goodness can be recovered by purifying the mind. When the will thus allows the mind to be true to its nature, knowledge of the good is naturally extended into action. Wang's doctrine gave the highest expression to idealistic Neo-Confucianism, which had its roots in the work of the 11th-century philosopher Cheng Hao and of Lu Jiuyuan, a 12th-century contemporary of Zhu Xi.

Back in public life in 1510 as a magistrate in Jiangxi, Wang continued working as a reformer. His innovations earned him an audience with the emperor, which was followed by a succession of appointments in higher levels of government. As governor of southern Jiangxi, he suppressed several rebellions and implemented governmental, social, and educational reform. In 1521 the emperor appointed him war minister and awarded him the title of earl of Xinjian.

After returning home to mourn the death of his father in 1522, Wang remained there for more than five years, meeting hundreds of his followers. His conversations with his disciples were compiled in *Chuanxilu* (*Instructions for Practical Living*), his main work.

In 1527 Wang journeyed to Guangxi to put down a rebellion. Having suffered for years from a chronic cough, which now became acute, Wang fell very ill. He died on his return from Guangxi in Nan'an, Jiangxi Province, in 1529.

Upon his death, a powerful minister who hated Wang had his earldom and other hereditary privileges revoked, disinheriting his two sons. Wang's so-called false teachings were also forbidden. However, in 1567, the new emperor honored Wang with the posthumous titles of Marquis of Xinjian and Completion of Culture. Beginning in 1584 he was offered sacrifice in the Confucian temple, the highest honor. For several generations after his death, Wang's philosophy predominated in China and also greatly influenced Japanese thought.

ALFRED NORTH WHITEHEAD

(b. 1861–d. 1947)

Alfred North Whitehead was born in Ramsgate, Kent, Eng., on Feb. 5, 1861. A 20th-century giant in philosophy, Alfred North Whitehead was a thinker whose interests ranged over virtually the whole of science and human experience. He was an educational reformer and an analyst of religion as well.

In his early years he was educated at home and at Sherborne School in Dorset. He entered Trinity College, Cambridge, in 1880 and remained there as student and teacher until 1910. In 1911 he was appointed to University College in London, and in 1914 he became professor of applied mathematics at the Imperial College of Science and Technology. In 1924, faced with the prospect of an unwanted retirement, Whitehead became professor of philosophy at Harvard University in Massachusetts.

Whitehead's earliest and most enduring interest was pure mathematics. He published *Treatise on Universal Algebra* in 1898. He abandoned the writing of a companion volume to work on one of the major treatises in the history of philosophy, *Principia Mathematica* (1910–13). His coauthor was Bertrand Russell, whom Whitehead considered the greatest logician in the history of philosophy. In 1911 Whitehead published *An Introduction to Mathematics* for a more general audience.

Dismayed at the quality of English schooling, he delivered a lecture in 1916 entitled "The Aims of Education," a brilliant attempt to reconcile general and special education. At the time he was attempting to construct the philosophical foundations of physics. The results were published as *Enquiry Concerning the Principles of Natural Knowledge* (1919). His major works while in the United States were *Science and the Modern World* (1925), *Religion in the Making* (1926), *Process and Reality* (1929), and *Adventures of Ideas* (1933), probably his most interesting book for the majority of readers.

Whitehead retired at age 76 but he remained at Harvard until his death on December 30, 1947.

BERNARD WILLIAMS
(b. 1929 – d. 2003)

Sir Bernard Williams, in full Sir Bernard Arthur Owen Williams, was on born Sep. 21, 1929, in Westcliff, Essex, Eng. He was noted especially for his writings on ethics and the history of Western philosophy, both ancient and modern.

Williams was educated at Chigwell School, Essex, and Balliol College, Oxford. During the 1950s he served in the Royal Air Force (1951–53) and was a fellow of All Souls College and New College, Oxford. He was appointed Knightbridge Professor of Philosophy at the University of Cambridge in 1967 and Provost of King's College, Cambridge, in 1979. He was Monroe Deutsch Professor of Philosophy at the University of California, Berkeley, from 1988 to 2003 and White's Professor of Moral Philosophy at Oxford from 1990 to 1996.

In 1955 Williams married Shirley Catlin, who, as Shirley Williams, became a prominent political figure in Britain; in 1993 she was created Baroness Williams of Crosby. In 1974 the marriage was dissolved, and Williams married Patricia Skinner. Williams headed or served on a number of public commissions, notably the Committee on Obscenity and Film Censorship (1977–79), and was a director of the English National Opera. He was knighted in 1999.

Williams was trained in classics and wrote memorably about Plato, Aristotle, and Greek moral consciousness, but he was also one of the most prolific and versatile philosophers of his time. His published works include writings on René Descartes (1596–1650), Friedrich Nietzsche (1844–1900), and Ludwig Wittgenstein (1889–1951) and important papers and books on personal identity, the relation of morality to human motivation, the idea of social and political equality, the nature and value of truth, the significance of death, and the role and limits of objectivity in science, morality, and human life. He did not put forward a systematic philosophical theory. He was suspicious of systematic theories, particularly in ethics, because in his view they failed to be true to the contingency, complexity, and individuality of human life.

Williams was recognized for his brilliance even as an undergraduate. He was trained in philosophy when Oxford was home to the new movement of linguistic analysis, or ordinary language philosophy, led by J.L. Austin, but the breadth of his cultural, historical, and political interests kept him from becoming an adherent of that school. He met its standards of clarity of expression and rigour in argument, but his aims in philosophy went far beyond conceptual analysis. He regarded philosophy as an effort to achieve a deeper understanding of human life and the human point of view in its multiple dimensions. For the same reasons, he also resisted the tendency to regard scientific knowledge as the model of understanding to which philosophy should aspire at a more abstract level—a tendency that was strengthened during his lifetime by the growing influence of the American philosopher W.V.O. Quine and by a shift in the center of gravity of English-language philosophy from Britain to the United States. Williams held that physical science could aspire to an objectivity and universality that did not make sense for humanistic subjects, and his greatest influence came from his challenge to the ambition of universality and objectivity in ethics, especially as expressed in utilitarianism but also in the tradition established by Immanuel Kant.

In his book *Descartes: The Project of Pure Inquiry* (1978), Williams gave a compelling description of the ideal of objectivity in science, which he called the "absolute conception" of reality. According to this conception, different human perspectives on and representations of the world are the product of interaction between human beings, as constituents of the world, and the world itself as an independently existing reality. Humans cannot apprehend the world except by some form of perception or representation; yet they can recognize, and to some extent identify and try to compensate for, the distortions or limitations that their own point of view and their relation to the rest of reality introduce. The aim of objectivity in science is by this method to approach as closely as possible to the absolute conception—a conception of what is there "anyway," independent of the human point of view. Historical self-consciousness about the contingent elements in this process is compatible with the idea of a single truth toward which humans are trying to make progress.

Williams was aware of the doubts that exist regarding whether this ideal is intelligible, let alone attainable, in light of the fact that human thinking must start from some particular historical moment and must use the contingent biological faculties and cultural tools that happen to be at hand. But whatever may be the difficulties in pursuing this ideal, he believed that it makes sense as an ambition. If there is a way things are anyway, then it makes sense to want to know what that way is and to explain the nature of human perceptions in terms of it.

Some philosophers, in the tradition of David Hume (1711–1776), have denied that there can be objective truth in ethics on the ground that this would have to mean, very implausibly, that moral propositions are true because they represent moral entities or structures that are part of the furniture of the world—moral realities with which humans have some kind of causal interaction, as they do with the physical objects of scientific knowledge. Williams was also doubtful about objectivity in ethics, but his criticism does not depend on this false analogy with science and is more interesting.

Moral judgments, according to Williams, are about what people should do and how they should live, they do not at all purport to represent how things are in the outside world. So, if there is any objectivity in moral judgments, it would have to be sought in a different analogy with scientific objectivity. Objective truth in ethics would have to consist not in ethical entities or properties added to the absolute conception of the external world but in the objective validity of the reasoning that supports certain practical, rather than descriptive, judgments about what people should do and how they should live. The analogy with scientific objectivity would reside in the fact that the way to arrive at such objective and universally valid truth would be to detect and correct for the biases and distortions introduced into one's practical judgment by contingencies of one's personal or parochial perspective. The more distortions one could correct, the closer one would get to the truth.

But it is just this aim, central to the idea of moral objectivity that Williams thinks is fundamentally misguided. Williams finds something bizarre about the theoretical ambition of discovering a standard for practical judgment that escapes the perspectival peculiarities of the individual point of view. This applies to any ethical theory with a strong basis in impartiality or with a claim to universal validity. Williams's basic point is that, in the practical domain, the ambition of transcending one's own point of view is absurd. If taken seriously, it is likely to be profoundly self-deceived in its application. To Williams, the ambition is akin to that of the person who tries to eliminate from his life all traces of the fact that it is his.

Williams developed this objection through his general view that practical reasons must be "internal" rather than "external": that is, reasons for action must derive from motives that a person already has; they cannot create new motives by themselves, through the force of reason alone. He also defended a limited form of ethical relativism. He believed that, while there can be ethical truth, it is local and historically contingent and based on reasons deriving from people's actual motives and practices, which are not timeless or universal. Consequently, moral judgments cannot be applied to cultures too far removed in time and character from the culture in which they originate.

These arguments appear in *Ethics and the Limits of Philosophy* (1985), *A Critique of Utilitarianism* (1973; in *Utilitarianism: For and Against*), and some of the essays reprinted in *Moral Luck* (1981) and *Making Sense of*

Humanity (1995). The debate provoked by Williams's claim that impersonal moral standards undermine the integrity of personal projects and personal relations, which give life its very meaning, was an important part of the moral and political philosophy of the later 20th century. Even philosophers who did not accept Williams's conclusions were in most cases led to recognize the importance of accommodating the personal point of view as a factor in moral theory.

Williams also raised and explored the deep question of whether a person's moral status is immune to "luck," or purely contingent circumstances, as Kant had argued (for Kant, the moral status of an individual depends only on the quality of his will). Williams invented the concept of "moral luck" and offered strong reasons to think that people are morally vulnerable to contingencies beyond their control, a conception he found exemplified in Greek tragedy. Oedipus, for example, is not relieved of guilt for killing his father and marrying his mother by the fact that he did not know at the time that that was what he was doing. Williams's remarkable philosophical-literary-historical work, *Shame and Necessity* (1993), presented these ideas in a rich study of Greek ethical thought.

Williams came to the conclusion that, instead of following the model of natural science, the project of understanding human nature should rely on history, which provides some distance from the perspective of the present without leaving the fullness of the human perspective behind. During the latter part of his career, this viewpoint coincided with his admiration for Nietzsche, whose genealogical method was an example of historical self-exploration. In Williams's last book, *Truth and Truthfulness* (2002), he applied these ideas to the importance of truth in the theoretical and practical spheres as well as in political and personal relations.

Williams's major published works, in addition to those mentioned above, include *Morality: An Introduction to Ethics* (1972); *Problems of the Self: Philosophical Papers* (1973); *In the Beginning Was the Deed: Realism and Moralism in Political Argument* (2005); *The Sense of the Past: Essays in the History of Philosophy* (2005); *Philosophy as a Humanistic Discipline* (2005); and *On Opera* (2006). Williams died on June 10, 2003, in Rome, Italy.

LUDWIG WITTGENSTEIN

(b. 1889–d. 1951)

L udwig Josef Johann Wittgenstein was born in Vienna, Austria, on April 26, 1889, the youngest child of a wealthy steelmaker. Twice in his lifetime Wittgenstein tried to solve all the problems of philosophy. His second attempt marked a criticism and rejection of his first, and in the end he regarded both as failures. A multitalented man, never at ease with himself or the world around him, he was, mathematician, engineer, architect, and musician. He pursued philosophical problems with zeal, yet he regarded nothing as ridiculous as to be a teacher of philosophy.

He was educated at home until age 14. He then studied mathematics, natural sciences, and engineering. In 1908 he went to England to engage in aeronautical research. In 1911 he attended Cambridge University to study with the English philosopher and mathematician Bertrand Russell. Wittgenstein served in the Austrian army during World War I, and by the end of the war he had finished his first major work, *Tractatus Logico-Philosophicus*, a 20th-century classic published in 1921.

In 1919 Wittgenstein gave away the fortune inherited from his father and worked as

Austrian philosopher Ludwig Wittgenstein. Photo Researchers/ Getty Images

a schoolteacher in small Austrian villages until 1925. For ten years he was not involved in philosophy, until 1929 when he returned to Cambridge as a lecturer. The product of his work there was *Philosophical Investigations*, which was published two years after his death.

The *Tractatus* is only 75 pages long. It consists of a series of remarks ordered and numbered in decimal notation. Its main focus is on language: every sentence that says something must be "a picture of reality." Things that cannot be pictured cannot be said because saying them means nothing. The endless variety of language conceals an underlying unity of truth. In *Investigations*, he rejects this concept. His emphasis became language as description, not a picture of reality. Language serves to dissolve confusion, not to discover essential truth. Wittgenstein passed away in Cambridge on April 19, 1951.

ZENO OF CITIUM

(b. 335 BCE – d. 263 BCE)

Zeno of Citium was born in 335 BCE, in Citium, Cyprus. He was a Greek thinker who founded the Stoic school of philosophy, which influenced the development of philosophical and ethical thought in Hellenistic and Roman times.

He went to Athens c. 312 BCE and attended lectures by the Cynic philosophers Crates of Thebes and Stilpon of Megara, in addition to lectures at the Academy. Arriving at his own philosophy, he began to teach in the Stoa Poikile (Painted Colonnade), whence the name of his philosophy. Zeno's philosophical system included logic and theory of knowledge, physics, and ethics—the latter being central. He taught that happiness lay in conforming the will to the divine reason, which governs the universe. In logic and the theory of knowledge he was influenced by Antisthenes and Diodorus Cronus, in physics by Heracleitus. None of his many treatises, written in harsh but forceful Greek, has survived save in fragmentary quotations.

Zeno of Citium died in 263 BCE, Athens.

ZENO OF ELEA

(b. 495 BCE–d. 430 BCE)

Z eno of Elea was a Greek philosopher and mathematician, whom Aristotle called the inventor of dialectic. Zeno is especially known for his paradoxes that contributed to the development of logical and mathematical rigor and that were insoluble until the development of precise concepts of continuity and infinity.

Zeno was famous for the paradoxes whereby, in order to recommend the Parmenidean doctrine of the existence of "the one" (i.e., indivisible reality), he sought to controvert the commonsense belief in the existence of "the many" (i.e., distinguishable qualities and things capable of motion). Zeno was the son of a certain Teleutagoras and the pupil and friend of Parmenides. In Plato's *Parmenides*, Socrates, "then very young," converses with Parmenides and Zeno, "a man of about forty," but it may be doubted whether such a meeting was chronologically possible. Plato's account of Zeno's purpose (*Parmenides*), however, is presumably accurate. In reply to those who thought that Parmenides' theory of the existence of "the one" involved inconsistencies, Zeno tried to show that the assumption of the existence of a plurality of things in time and space carried with it more serious inconsistencies. In early youth he collected his arguments in a book, which, according to Plato, was put into circulation without his knowledge.

Zeno made use of three premises: first, that any unit has magnitude. Second, that it is infinitely divisible, and third, that it is indivisible. Yet he incorporated arguments for each: for the first premise, he argued that that which, added to or subtracted from something else, does not increase or decrease the second unit is nothing; for the second, that a unit, being one, is homogeneous and that therefore, if divisible, it cannot be divisible at one point rather than another. For the third, that a unit, if divisible, is divisible either into extended minima, which contradicts the second premise or, because of the first premise, into nothing. He had in his hands a very powerful complex argument in the form of a dilemma, one horn of which supposed indivisibility, the other infinite

132

divisibility, both leading to a contradiction of the original hypothesis. His method had great influence and may be summarized as follows: he continued Parmenides' abstract, analytic manner but started from his opponents' theses and refuted them by reductio ad absurdum. It was probably the two latter characteristics which Aristotle had in mind when he called him the inventor of dialectic.

That Zeno was arguing against actual opponents, Pythagoreans who believed in a plurality composed of numbers that were thought of as extended units, is a matter of controversy. It is not likely that any mathematical implications received attention in his lifetime. But in fact the logical problems which his paradoxes raise about a mathematical continuum are serious, fundamental, and inadequately solved by Aristotle.

ZHUANGZI

(b. c. 369 – d. 286 BCE)

Zhuangzi was a Chinese philosopher, author, and teacher. He was extremely influential in the development of Chinese philosophy and religious thought. Zhuangzi interpreted Daoism (from *dao*, "way") differently from Laozi.

Zhuangzi taught that wise people accept the ebb and flow of life without attempting to challenge it and that true enlightenment involves freeing oneself of traditions and personal goals that stand in the way of the mysterious, all-encompassing Dao.

ZHU XI

(b. 1130–d. 1200)

Zhu Xi was born on Oct. 18, 1130, in Youxi, Fujian Province, China. With his interpretation of the teachings of Confucius and his followers, Zhu Xi shaped people's understanding of Confucianism from the 13th century onward. The *Sishu* (*Four Books*), which includes teachings of Confucius and his disciple Mencius and commentaries by Zhu Xi, was for centuries the central text for both primary education and the civil service examinations in China. It has had a greater influence on Chinese culture than any other text.

Zhu Xi was educated in the Confucian tradition by his father, a local official. He passed the highest civil service examination at the age of 18, when the average age for such an accomplishment was 35. In his first official position, he served as a registrar in Tongan from 1151 to 1158. There he reformed the taxation and police systems, improved the standard of the local school, and drew up a code of proper formal conduct and ritual.

After his assignment at Tongan ended, Zhu Xi did not accept another official appointment for more than 20 years. He was dissatisfied with the men in power and their policies, and he preferred the life of a teacher and scholar. He continued his involvement in public affairs, however, by expressing his political views in memorandums addressed to the emperor.

Meanwhile, Zhu had become committed to Neo-Confucianism. He had studied with Li Tong, one of the ablest followers of the 11th-century Neo-Confucian philosophers. In their attempt to regain the intellectual preeminence that Confucianism had lost to Daoism and Buddhism in previous centuries, the Neo-Confucians had created a new metaphysical system applying Confucian principles to questions regarding the fundamental nature of reality.

Zhu Xi's philosophy synthesized important concepts that had been developed by earlier Neo-Confucians. Like them, Zhu Xi held that the universe has two aspects: the formless and the formed. The formless, or *li*, is a principle or a network of principles that determines the nature of all things. The *qi*, or material force, brings physical form to the li and serves to explain the existence of individuals, change, and creation.

Zhu Xi carried out a rewarding exploration of ideas through both his formal writings and his correspondence with friends and scholars of differing views. In 1175, for instance, he and fellow Neo-Confucian Lu Jiuyuan engaged in a famous debate on the issue of perfecting the mind. In contrast to Lu's insistence on meditation as the exclusive means of achieving spiritual growth, Zhu Xi emphasized the value of inquiry and study of external reality, including book learning.

Zhu Xi completed his commentaries on the *Lunyu* (*Analects*) of Confucius and the *Mencius* in 1177. In 1188 he wrote an important commentary on *Daxue* (*Great Learning*), a text on moral government attributed to Confucius and his disciple Zengzi. Confucius's assertion that the emperor could accomplish the moral transformation of the world by first cultivating his own mind was an idea to which Zhu Xi returned repeatedly in his

Sculpture depicting the Confucian scholar and philosopher Zhu Xi, at Mount Wuyi, Fujian Province, China. Hiroshi Higuchi/Photographer's Choice/ Getty Images

writings. He completed a commentary on the *Zhongyong* (*Doctrine of the Mean*) in 1189. The following year Zhu Xi published these four texts, along with his commentaries on them, as the *Sishu*.

Zhu Xi was an outspoken and uncompromising critic of Chinese politics. Near the end of his life, he was barred from political activity, and he was still in political disgrace when he died on April 23, 1200.

Zhu Xi's reputation was restored soon after his death, and in 1241 his memory was honored with the placement of his tablet in the Confucian Temple. Ironically, in the 1310s, his philosophical system was officially adopted by a government more authoritarian than those he had so vehemently criticized. In Korea the Choson, or Yi, Dynasty (1392–1910) also adopted Zhu Xi's Neo-Confucianism as the state ideology, and his philosophy spread in Japanese society during the Tokugawa period (1603–1867).

GLOSSARY

ABSOLUTISM A political theory that absolute power should be vested in one or more rulers.

DOCTRINE A set of ideas or beliefs that are taught or believed to be true.

EXISTENTIALISM A chiefly 20th century philosophical movement centering on analysis of individual existence and the nature of free will.

JURISPRUDENCE The science or philosophy of law.

LINGUISTICS The study of human speech including the units, nature, structure, and modification of language.

MAXIM A well-known phrase that expresses a general truth about life or a rule about behaviour.

MEDITATIVE Very thoughtful.

METAPHYSICS A study of what is outside objective experience. This division of philosophy is concerned with the fundamental nature of reality and being.

MILITIA A part of the organized armed forces of a country liable to be called upon only in emergency.

NIHILISM The belief that traditional morals, ideas, or beliefs have no worth or value.

PACIFISM An attitude or policy of nonresistance.

PARALLELISM A theory that mind and matter accompany one another but are not causally related.

POSITIVISM A philosophical doctrine that rejects pure speculation and says that scientific knowledge is the only true form of knowledge.

PRACTITIONER A person who regularly does an activity that requires skill or practice.

SPATIAL Relating to, involving, or having the nature of space.

STOIC A member of the school of philosophy emphasizing the pursuit of knowledge unhindered by excessive emotion.

FOR MORE INFORMATION

American Philosophical Society (APS)
104 South Fifth Street
Philadelphia, PA 19106
Web site: http://www.amphilsoc.org
The American Philosophical Society promotes knowledge in the sciences and humanities through research, professional meetings, publications, library resources, and community outreach. The APS has played an important role in American cultural and intellectual life for over 250 years.

Canadian Philosophical Association
Saint Paul University
223 Main Street
Ottawa, ON K1S 1C4 Canada
(613) 236-1393, ext. 2454
Web site: http://www.acpcpa.ca
The Canadian Philosophical Association was founded in 1958 to promote philosophical scholarship and education across Canada and to represent the interests of the profession in public forums. It is bilingual and publishes a quarterly journal called *Dialogue*.

Canadian Society for History and Philosophy of Mathematics (CSHPM)
Quest University
Squamish, BC V8B 0N8 Canada
Web site: http://www.cshpm.org
The CSHPM, founded in 1974, promotes research and teaching in the history and philosophy of mathematics. It meets once a year and publishes a biannual bulletin.

Institute for American Religious and Philosophical Thought (IARPT)
3916 Linden Terrace
Durham, NC 27705
(336) 334-4912
Web site: www.hiarpt.org
The IARPT contributes to the study of religion and philosophy and focuses mainly on American religious philosophy and thought.

Prior to June, 2012, the organization was known as The Highlands Institute.

Metaphysical Society of America
Gonzaga University
CE Box 47 502 E. Boone Avenue
Spokane WA 99258
(509) 313-5885
Web site: http://www.metaphysicalsociety.org
The Metaphysical Society of America is an organization of professional philosophers that meets once annually to discuss issues of fundamental concern to all of the major areas of philosophy.

Society for the Advancement of American Philosophy (SAAP)
c/o Department of Philosophy, Box 179
University of Colorado at Denver
P.O. Box 173364
Denver, CO 80217-3364
(303) 556-8558
Web site: http://www.american-philosophy.org
SAAP's aim is to advance American philosophy by promoting interest and research in its history, encouraging original and creative work , and providing forums for the exchange of information and ideas.

FOR FURTHER READING

Chin, Annping. *The Authentic Confucius: A Life of Thought and Politics.* New York, NY: Scribner, 2007.

Chomsky, Noam, and David Barsamian. *What We Say Goes: Conversations on US Power in a Changing World.* New York, NY: Metropolitan Books, 2007.

Leibniz, Gottfried Wilhelm. *Protogea.* London, England: University of Chicago Press Ltd., 2008.

Locke, John. *Two Treatises of Government and a Letter Concerning Toleration.* New York, NY: Classic Books International, 2010.

Moseley, Alexander. *A to Z of Philosophy.* London, England: Continuum International Publishing Group, 2008.

Needleman, Jacob, and John Piazza. *Essential Marcus Aurelius.* New York, NY: Penguin Group, 2008.

Nietzsche, Friedrich. *Thus Spoke Zarathustra.* Hollywood, FL: Simon and Brown, 2012.

Peppiatt, Michael. *Francis Bacon: Anatomy of an Enigma.* London, England: Constable & Robinson Ltd., 2008.

Pyke, Steve. *Philosophers.* New York, NY: Oxford University Press, 2011.

Sperber, Johnathan. *Karl Marx: A Nineteenth-Century Life.* New York, NY: Liveright Publishing, 2013.

INDEX